[handwritten inscription] Legn, from the best Bill Bonnstetter

What I Know Now

Bill J. Bonnstetter

Forbes

CUSTOM PUBLISHING

60 FIFTH AVE · NEW YORK, NY · 10011

CIP Data is available.
Printed in Canada.
10 9 8 7 6 5 4 3 2 1

ISBN 0–8281–1420–x

Dedication

My parents lost a lot of sleep worrying about me the first 30 years of my life—they just didn't understand what I was about—and, I, in turn, didn't understand their satisfaction with such a small world as the farm, family, and town. We lived in the same place but could have been on different planets.

As I grew older and wiser in my understanding of self and others, my parents' world became a beautiful revelation to me—they worked hard to keep the farm going, they loved and respected their children, and the loss of sleep over my adventures never altered their love and respect for me. As a man in my fifties returning to visit them, it was my joy to see their eyes light up when I asked to take a walk around the farm, asked after an ailing neighbor, shared their quiet dinner around the kitchen table—you see, unwittingly, it was my parents and their loving patience that gave me the opportunity to be different and grow with that difference.

My wife and caring companion, Karen, continues that same loving patience and respect for my differences even at this time in my life. She doesn't always understand "why," but she respects my "need to do" that keeps me going.

My two sons, Dave and Matt, are now teaching me to use all the tools talked about in my book—to honor their differences and be proud of them for their strength to live them out.

A c k n o w l e d g m e n t s

People don't know what they know until the words are gathered to articulate the knowledge. This book took years of research and formulation before it could be written. My appreciation and thanks go to many people who helped me understand myself, others, and our environment—making it possible to discover the words that would let me describe *"What I Know Now."*

Gratefully I would like to acknowledge my associate, Randy J. Widrick, who contributed many hours and ideas to this book. Some of the other colleagues whom I have collaborated with over the years, and who encouraged me to continue the project, are Judy Suiter, Jon Hall, Robert Alderman, John Mathis, and Dr. Russ Watson. They, and many others who form a roster too long to list, have my gratitude. I thank you all.

Bill J. Bonnstetter

Bill Bonnstetter is the founder and President of TTI Performance Systems, Ltd. marketing products in the United States and Canada. His company, Success Insights, Ltd., operates in over 40 countries. He is the author of over thirty software programs; many of these have been translated into over twenty languages.

He has co-authored numerous training programs including: Building High Performance Teams, Behavioral Selling Skills, Energizing The Organization, Dynamic Customer Satisfaction, The Universal Language DISC, a Reference Manual and Sales Strategy Index. His company has now transferred many of these programs to CD with audio. Over three million people throughout the world have utilized the software and training programs.

Bill has a passion for research and he continuously searches for new ways to help people understand themselves and others. He recently received a patent on a software program that integrates values and behavior and is doing extended research on principles and beliefs.

Bill surrounds himself with consultants and a staff that is kept busy keeping up with his new ideas and innovations. He is a man who "has strong self-efficacy" (a word you will meet in this book on many occasions) and the energy of three people.

C o n t e n t s

1

I Was Different, Too

It's never too late to learn. That's a phrase we have all heard many times over. I have learned more about myself in the last five years than I learned in the previous fifty-five years. Can you say that?

From a very early age, I knew I was different.

Why I was different didn't really concern me. I was pretty happy with myself. My hair was red—but my mother and sister had red hair too. No big deal. But, then, someone told me that redheads were always quick to anger. So, I became quite good at being "quick to anger." It never occurred to me that my older sister and my mother (both redheads, remember) did not have this same characteristic.

I began to examine my differences and a number of questions began to form. My guess is that you, too, have asked yourself some of these same questions:

- Why did my mother always think that my friends were the reason I got in trouble?
- Why did I get punished for things that I didn't think were punishable actions?
- Why did my teachers pick on me?
- Why did everyone remember all the "naughty" things I'd done and remind me of them for years?
- Why did my mother lose so much sleep wondering why I did what I did?

- Why did my father put up with my mischievous behavior as long as I continued to do my share of the farm work each day?

I grew up on a farm in Corwith, Iowa. Iowa is the heart of the farm belt and as a result, a lot of people in our community lived on farms. In fact, most of my classmates lived on farms. So, what made me different from them? More questions formed in my mind:

- Why was I different from my older brother and sister—they rarely got in trouble.
- Why did I see things differently from my parents and siblings?
- Why did I stand out in a crowd?
- Why did I leave home the day after graduating from high school?
- Why did I always date girls from another town when in high school? In fact, why wouldn't the local girls date me?
- Why did I marry someone I had only known for 18 days?
- Why did I confine my hometown visits to very short stays after leaving home?
- Why, when I went home, did I get so bored with all the small talk about the price of corn and the weather?
- Why did the visits with my family totally change when I showed interest in "their world of the farm"?
- Why did it take me eight years to receive my first degree? Why did I keep going?
- Why didn't I like the Army?
- Why did the Army's GI Bill pay me more money to go to school than they paid me to serve full time?
- Why did I resent being told when to get up, what to wear, and what to do when I was in the Army?
- Why did I have the same difficulty understanding my own kids that my parents had with me?
- Why have I been so successful in my business career?
- Why did my youngest son always think that I treated his brother better than him?
- Why do I break rules?

- Why do I get mad when people want to talk about spending money on aesthetics?

Knowing the answers to these questions would have benefited myself and all the other people in my life.

When people lack the ability to articulate their true feelings and passions, it leads to potential relationship problems and poor career choices. For the past twenty years, my goal has been to help people understand themselves and others. The questionnaires that I have designed do just that. They are validated assessments that provide feedback to help people truly understand themselves.

2

Each of Us is Unique— We Can't be Cloned

I am a visual person. No matter where I have traveled in this world, it has always been amazing to me to notice the infinite varieties of flowers, plants, and trees. The assortment of colors, shapes, sizes, and aromas enhances this world we live in. From the saguaro cactus of Arizona to the maple trees of New York, every diverse plant has found its own place to grow, a place where the nourishment it needs comes from the climate and soil. Each one of these different growing plants possesses its own uniqueness. We naturally appreciate the uniqueness of the foliage, and we know that certain plants grow best in certain environments. The diversity of the plant kingdom greatly enhances its beauty. The combination of colors, shapes, and smells combine to create beautiful floral arrangements that decorate our homes and offices.

What would the world be like if only one flower existed—let's say, a rose. No daffodils, lilies, daisies, violets, dandelions, or marigolds. Just roses. Only roses. All flower shops would be called "Rose Shops." Let's go one step farther; the only color of rose would be red. No white, yellow, or all the other pretty colors. Imagine this and you see how much we appreciate variety. Remember the saying, *variety is the spice of life.*

Imagine the life of a dog. It eats the same dog food day after day. We complain about leftovers! We love variety in food and in animals, right? Some people own St. Bernards; others prefer dachshunds, chows, or shepherds. We *love* variety and we *seek out* variety. Imagine a restaurant that only served one item, whatever the "daily special" was for that day. Can you imagine? Maybe they called it the "meat loaf house" and guess what's for dinner. No, thank you. I prefer variety. One night I might crave Italian food, the next you'll find me at a Mexican restaurant. Variety *is* what makes life exciting and fun. We appreciate variety in everything — except people.

With people, we call it *diversity*. Just for discussion, let's say the following equation is true:

$$\boxed{\text{Diversity} = \text{Variety}}$$

Isn't it interesting? That which we desire, value and expect in animals, food, cars, clothing, flowers, houses, vacations, jewelry and virtually everything you can imagine—we criticize in people. With people, we tend to be harsher in our judgements.

That's what this book is all about. My research validates that people view the world differently. These differences are neither right nor wrong. Just different. If you understand the different views, you can positively enhance your personal life and the life of others. In seminars I have taught all over the world, I see the same reaction when this subject comes up. People bow their heads downward with a small guilty smile as they realize that they have been too harsh on others, too judgmental or unappreciative of the beauty in the differences of others. Thousands of people have experienced the power of the material I have developed that helps them understand these differences and they have walked away with a new appreciation of "the flower garden of humanity."

That is what I see. Humanity as a beautiful flower garden! Unlimited variety, sizes, shapes, colors and personalities enhance that garden. It is to be appreciated, nurtured and observed. We can learn from others and enhance our own lives if we look at people with more open and accepting eyes. When all is said and done, and we're sitting back in that rocking chair—the greatest possession we can reflect on is how we touched other lives throughout the years, the relationships we have built, and the friendships we have shared.

So, let's begin our journey. Let's begin with you understanding you. Let's answer some of those unanswered questions you have lived with all your life *to this point.* Lao Tse said, "He who understands others is learned, he who understands himself is wise." Let's go for *wise* before *learned.*

First we will discuss a few basic truths, then we'll move on to my research and how it applies to you and your interaction with others.

Basic Truths

Truth 1:   You are unique!
Truth 2:   You can't be cloned!
Truth 3:   You can be the champion of your own life!

Truth 1: You are unique!

You are special. You are prized. You are one of a kind—unique. Designed to achieve and accomplish great and awesome things. There is no one else like you. Look around at everyone. Is there anyone just like you? Does anyone look or act as you do? I think not.

Some are vertically challenged (a little politically correct phrasing . . .) and others are horizontally challenged. Some of us are just short and others are, well . . . not as slender as we could be. We are all uniquely different. And, that is what makes us each wonderful.

Excuse me, do you mind if I clone you?

Whoa! And now we hear talk of cloning. Someone may approach you one day and say, "I want to clone you." Impossible. It can't happen. Sure, someone can create a physical look-alike, but no one can clone the part of you that's really you. Your mother's body chemistry would need to be an exact replica of when you were in the womb. Some research suggests that outside environment has an effect on the baby before birth, so this variable would have to be duplicated as well. After your entrance into the world, every interaction and relationship would have to occur at the identical point of time and each response would have to be repeated exactly— after all, we are looking for a perfect match. You see, in order to duplicate you, we must totally replicate the billions of interactions you have had throughout your life, which is absolutely impossible.

Just for fun, let's suppose we could clone you. Your clone would have to respond to every single circumstance in the same way you did. Life is crowded with choices. Pause a moment and remember a few of those tough choices you faced. Maybe sometimes you chose right and sometimes wrong. What would your clone choose? Would your reputation be ruined? Your name damaged? All because some "you-wannabe" made the wrong choices.

Truth 2: You can't be cloned.

There will never be another one like you. Your entrance into this world, your journey through it and your exit from it make a statement of who you are and what you believe. Your choices will determine your destiny. You are you!

The uniqueness of you is what this book is all about. So much of society seems to want to rob you of YOU; telling you what you can't do and how you can't succeed. Telling you that you are not valuable and that you can't achieve greatness—telling you through words, actions, and gestures that you are a ZERO when in fact—you can be the champion of your life!

Truth 3: You can be the champion of your life.

A champion? Yes, and again louder, YES! History is replete with examples of men and women who overcame tremendous odds and made a difference. You have the potential to do just that. The only person holding you back is you. The greatest obstacle to your success is your belief system. You are the runner in the race of your life. I can't win it for you, but, I can point you in the right direction.

Throughout our lives, we hear others tell us what we can or cannot do, whether we are right or wrong, normal or abnormal. With the knowledge in this book, I am going to put YOU in control. You will make better decisions about your life and career. You will understand how you think and appreciate who you are. With this new self-awareness, you will appreciate the differences in how others view the world. You will better understand causes of conflict and be able to be a mediator. In other words, if you apply it, this book will dramatically change your life. You are uniquely you, and, that is wonderful.

Interactions with the following questions will make you think and will increase your learning.

1. I said earlier that we desire and crave variety in all areas of life except in people. We tend to harshly judge people who are different than ourselves. Do you agree? Think of two examples.

2. Many companies still utilize the assembly line. When a worker continually does the same repetitive work, what message does that send to the worker about his or her worth?

3. What have people done for you that made you feel unique and special?

4. What have people done for you or how have they acted toward you that made you feel more like a zero?

5. On the scale below, how do you generally feel about yourself?

Zero   **Champion**
Loser   **Winner**
Not Valued   **Prized**

6. If you placed yourself closer to the Champion side, why?

7. If you placed yourself closer to the Zero side, why do you feel that way?

Regardless of where you placed yourself on the scale, my goal is to continually have you moving toward the champion side, continually increasing your self-esteem. Whether you realize it or not, you have control over the above scale. You can move yourself to the winning side. I'll show you how in later chapters.

3

Subconsciously Speaking

An old proverb states, "As a man thinketh in his heart, so is he." Great thinkers and researchers throughout the ages have continually noted the power of beliefs.

I once heard of a music teacher who, when his students were struggling with a difficult piece and said, "I can't play it," would always respond the same way: "Can't never did anything!"

Another wise person said: "Those who say it can't be done are usually interrupted by those doing it." Mary Kay Ashe, the founder of Mary Kay Cosmetics, traditionally gives her beauty consultants a bumblebee pin. Why? Aerodynamically a bumblebee should not be able to fly. The mass of the body is too big for the wings to carry it. Please, the next time you're outside and see the bumblebee, don't tell her, she'll fall right on the ground.

I once knew a man who owned a blade sharpening business. Living on a windy hilltop, he believed he could harness the power of the wind to run his blade sharpener. His theory was that he could reduce his electrical cost by 50 percent by building a windmill. You've never seen a windmill like this one! It would start spinning vertically, then as the power of the wind increased, the speed of the turning blades would lift it to a horizontal helicopter-like spin. The power of the windmill would charge a series of batteries and those batteries would run the grinder for the blade sharpener. Excitedly he took his plans to one of the major universities in the United States. After the "experts" looked at the plans, they intelligently told him that the windmill would never work. Oh, well. Those who say it can't be done are usually interrupted by those doing it. The windmill worked wonderfully, just like the bumblebee. Actually, the "experts" saw it working also and believed he must have altered the plans. They were unwilling to accept the evidence before their eyes.

In the previous chapter, I stated my belief that you are unique. Whatever you do, you will add your own stamp to it. No one will walk your path in life; no one will do things exactly like you. You can't be cloned. You can be the champion of your own life, no matter what area you choose. Say it, here and now, out loud:

I can be the champion of my life!

Good! Say it often. You have within your subconscious a series of beliefs, positive and negative, about yourself and the world around you. Throughout your development, these beliefs have formed and shaped who you are. Some of your beliefs are strong and powerful. If challenged, you will defend them passionately. Other beliefs are weaker in their intensity; you may be positive, negative or even indifferent. Let's see, with the following little test. Answer 1–10 for each statement.

Activity 1

Personal Statements:

1. I believe I am a very attractive person.

   1   2   3   4   5   6   7   8   9   10
   No, I don't believe that   I strongly agree

2. I can achieve anything I desire.

   1   2   3   4   5   6   7   8   9   10
   No, I don't believe that   I strongly agree

3. I am unique, one of a kind. I can be my own champion.

   1   2   3   4   5   6   7   8   9   10
   No, I don't believe that   I strongly agree

4. Truth is mightier than the sword.

   1   2   3   4   5   6   7   8   9   10
   No, I don't believe that   I strongly agree

5. Education is the answer to the crime problem.

   1   2   3   4   5   6   7   8   9   10
   No, I don't believe that   I strongly agree

6. He who ends up with the most toys wins.

1	2	3	4	5	6	7	8	9	10

No, I don't believe that   I strongly agree

Are your answers different from mine? Suppose we were both on a committee to decide how much money should be spent on education related to crime prevention. Would we agree? Not necessarily, but that doesn't make me right and you wrong. And, guess what? It also doesn't mean that you are right and I am wrong. I value different things in life than you do. I see the world a different way than you do. My world view places a high value on things which you may not value at all. This is not a question of right and wrong. It is reality. We, as humans, tend to turn it into right and wrong.

Your beliefs are probably totally different from mine. The intensity of your beliefs are different from mine. You are different from me. We all know this, but we tend to turn it into a right-wrong issue, instead of learning to understand and appreciate one another.

Let's take a look at our subconscious again. We said it contains beliefs—positive, negative, and indifferent of varying intensities. Visually, let's say it looks like this:

Subconcious Mind

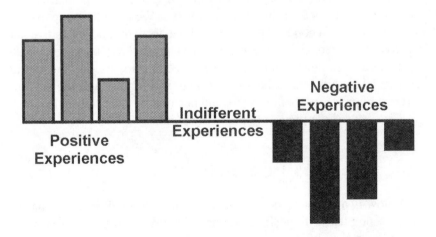

On the negative side of your subconscious are a multitude of beliefs, strong and weak in intensity. On the other side of the subconscious are the positive beliefs you value. When you experience (see, hear, feel, smell, or taste) something, your response to it falls somewhere instantly on the line above, either a valued positive response or a devalued negative response. In other words, you will instantly value or devalue an experience.

Here's a personal example: When my boys were growing up, there were occasions when the whole family would play charades in the evening. The marvelous thing about a game like charades is the great amount of laughter it can evoke as you do some very inventive kinds of things to communicate the message to your team. It also puts the entire group—adults, children, or both—all at the same level. We had a great time being together and sharing those times. I valued it immensely and as I listen to them reminisce about those evenings, I know they, too, placed a high value on those times and experiences.

In my business career, I emphasize the importance of taking time for the family. When I observe an associate overly committed to the job, I encourage that person to prioritize family time.

Now, on the negative side. I have had first-hand experience with people who, being so committed to the rules of their religion, are incredibly intolerant of others. Whether I experience such an intolerance personally, or see others victimized by it, I respond negatively—believing strongly that it is hurtful to humanity and wrong.

What about the "mystery of first impressions"? They have always intrigued me. Where do they come from? We'd like to think that we take time to think things over, but let's be realistic. We form first impressions instantly. In milliseconds, we attach a whole array of labels, positive and negative, to a person. As we meet a new person, we hear, see, shake hands, and even smell (hopefully perfume or cologne). A bewildering array of data hits our subconscious and is instantly catalogued into different impressions, both positive and negative.

Let's have some fun just to prove my point.

Activity 2

Below is a list of names. These random names will instantly flash a picture, complete with positive and negative brush strokes to your mind. Just follow a few simple rules:

1. Take a couple of seconds with each name and wait for a face to pop into your mind.

2. Take a few more seconds and notice how you feel about that face whose image has surfaced in your mind's eye. Good? Bad? Indifferent?

Rachel	Jonathan	Oprah
David	Vickie	Heather
Bill	Fred	Jamie
Karen	Rick	Bubba
Keith	Harold	Jackie
Matt	Jill	Linda

Did any evoke a very positive response? A negative response? Why?

Activity 3

Let's do the same thing with some sports—same rules apply.

Golf	Hockey	Pool
Bowling	Baseball	Swimming
Basketball	Track	Polo
Horse Racing	Auto Racing	Ping-Pong
Tennis		

Are you concerned that I left out your favorite sport? Where's that coming from? In fact, I could ask you to write or talk about your sport or favorite activity and you would talk about it passionately, from your perspective, your beliefs.

Let's take this thought a step further. Suppose you and I are at a party, talking to a group of mutual acquaintances and I make the following statement: "Crime could be totally solved and eliminated if we would spend more money on education. People who are educated will knowingly turn away from crime and drugs. That's where our money should go."

Would you agree or disagree with me? Would you argue with me? Would you even care that I made such a statement?

What's happening? You hear and see me make this argument. All of these impressions interact with the belief statements in your subconscious. In milliseconds each belief submits its information and a response is formulated. The intensity of your response will depend on the intensity of the beliefs supplying the information. Your response will be positive, negative or indifferent.

Here are two possible responses:

1. I don't agree with that at all. Crime is not associated with just the uneducated. Some of the most educated people in the world have used their brains to rip people off. I don't think education is the answer. We need tougher laws. (You may say this out loud to me or just think it quietly to yourself).

2. You think, "This guy's a loser, I'm outta here." Then you gradually slip off and look for more interesting conversations.

We have written on our subconscious a series of positive and negative beliefs of varying intensities. These are formed throughout our developmental stages and, if we are open-minded, can be altered throughout our life stages. These beliefs relate to how we value life.

Just how are these beliefs formed? (See Graph on next page).

Let's go back to the subconscious again. It is like a computer hard drive loaded with data. Where does the data come from to create our beliefs? Primarily, it comes from the outside world through our senses—seeing, hearing, touching, tasting, and smelling. Where else could the data come from? It is possible that we are born with a certain amount of data already on the "hard drive." What part of you is heredity and genetics, and what part of your make-up is the result of your environment? I believe nature (heredity) and nurture (environment) "dance together" to design the uniqueness of you. Heredity led the "dance" before you were born, but since your entrance into the world, I'm not sure which leads and which follows.

Possible Way Beliefs Are Formed

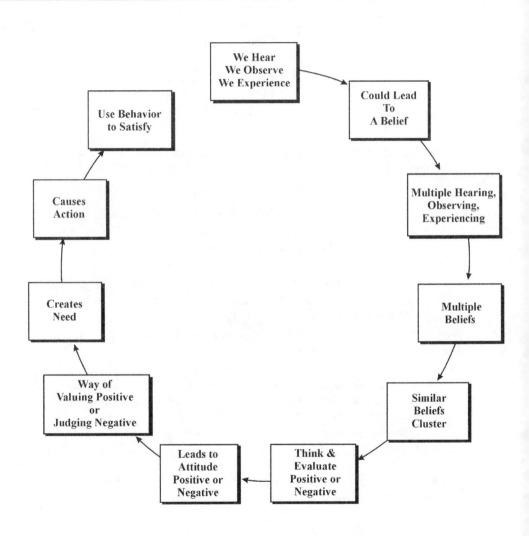

Let's all agree that genes have an impact on the development of the person. Our objective is not to argue how much or how little. We'll leave that to others to decide. In terms of the subconscious, the data enters primarily through the outside world, through the windows of our senses.

> **I hear**
> **I see**
> **I touch**
> **I smell**
> **I taste**

For easier explanation, I am going to categorize the five senses into one statement:

> **I experience**

I experience something through hearing-seeing-touching-smelling-and tasting. The data from that experience is processed by my mind. Impressions are formed, and these lead to beliefs. The degree of their intensity depends directly on the intensity of the experience.

Let's say that I have no information as to what a dog is like. I am, for this example, a very little boy:

> My mother takes me to my Grandma's house. I like going to my Grandma's house. When I get there, this warm and furry thing licks me and plays with me. It's like the stuffed animal on my bed, but it moves. I can pick it up and squeeze it. It makes noises. I like it. My mommy tells me it's a doggy. I like doggy.

What happened? I experienced, through my five senses, a dog. This positive experience sends data to my subconscious in a category called "dog."

What might I believe now about "dog"?

- Dog is furry.
- Dog smells funny.

- Dog likes me.
- I like dog.
- Dog is warm and licks my face.
- Dog is nice.
- When I pull dog's tail, it makes a noise from the front.
- When I squeeze dog it sometimes squirts on me.

I could make a universal statement here. There is only one dog in the world and he lives at my Grandma's house. We do that, don't we? We have one experience and turn it into a universal truth for all humanity.

Let's continue with my story:

Now as Mother pushes me in my stroller, back toward home, she runs into a friend of hers. He's got furry stuff on his face. It tickles when he kisses me. He's not a dog, though. He didn't lick me either. As he holds me, I see this big furry thing next to him that looks a lot like my Grandma's dog. Oh my! There is another dog besides my Grandma's. This one is bigger, a lot bigger. He has wet stuff running all down his mouth.

He's not the same color as my Grandma's. His hair is longer, too. I like him. His name is St. Bernard. He licked me, but that wet stuff from his mouth doesn't taste very good. He plays with me, but it hurts because he is so big and I'm so little. I cried, but I like him.

Now, I am getting really wise. I have more experience with dogs. Even though I'm little, I'm becoming a dog expert. What, with my new information, might I believe about dogs?

- There are two dogs.
- One is big. The other is little.
- Both lick my face, but one has water running out of his mouth, even though it doesn't taste like water.
- I like my Grandma's dog better. He doesn't hurt me.
- I like dogs.
- People can grow hair on their face, but it's not as soft as the dog's hair.

Any subsequent experience I have with dogs adds more data to my subconscious, altering my beliefs about dogs. In this case, my experience with dogs is positive. I value dogs. I will probably want to own a dog my entire life. When I see dogs that are the same breed as my Grandma's, it will trigger a positive response. Stated simply:

"I value dogs."

Earlier, I drew a simple picture of the subconscious. Let's go back to it.

Subconcious Mind

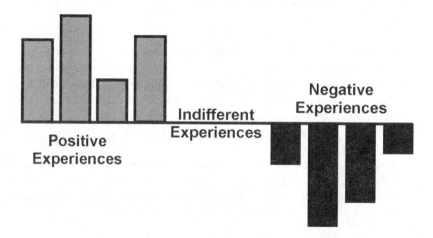

The experiences I had with dogs will lead to a positive valuing of dogs. When I see a dog, it will instantly trigger a positive response. If I see a dog like my Grandma's, it will instantly trigger a response of higher intensity, because of the higher intensity of the experience with Grandma's dog and the frequency of that positive experience (assuming I went to grandma's house often).

Let's create a different scenario. You fill in the beliefs.

Activity 4

1. Your first experience with a dog; you saw a dog growling and chasing a little girl or boy about your age.

   • What do you believe about dogs?

2. You were riding your bike; three dogs barked and chased after you. You were really scared.

   • What do you believe about dogs?

Let's put this all together. In your subconscious, based on the frequency and intensity of your experiences, you will have a multitude of beliefs classified into categories. Researchers tend to agree that similar beliefs cluster together. In other words, to play a bit with a familiar saying: "Beliefs of a feather—stick together." When we list the categories, you will tend to place a value on it, either positive, negative, or indifferent. Your subconscious might look like this:

Subconcious Mind

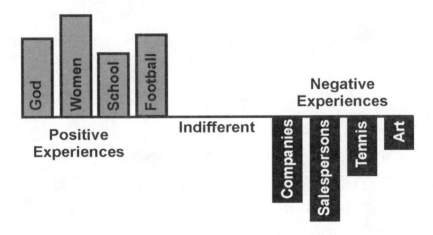

Within each of the categories in your subconscious is a series of beliefs. The overall weight of the experiences you have had will lead to a negative, positive, or indifferent viewpoint related to that category. For example, after numerous experiences with dogs, I decide I really like chows and terriers. I do not necessarily value shepherds or dobermans. But overall, I value dogs. The weight of the evidence, or rather, the weight of the *experiences* I have had, results in a positive value on dogs.

Another example: I may, due to my experience, not trust companies, as a general rule. However, I may work for a company that is small and family oriented. I still don't trust companies, but I trust this one. As it becomes larger, I begin to be concerned because it becomes less and less like a family and more like a company—or my (negative) picture of a company. I begin to move from a positive valuing (family) to a negative devaluing or not valuing (company). As long as the company acted like a family, I valued it immensely.

How many times have you found yourself believing a statement because it was authenticated by a doctor or a professor from a noted university? This can be an erroneous belief because the claims made may or may not be true. And then, there are the self-limiting beliefs—such as, believing that you are making more money than you deserve.

Our subconscious is chock-full of beliefs. I have explained how they are formed and organized. Oh, how powerful they are, and how they affect our actions. In the next chapter, we'll discuss how your beliefs can hinder you from achieving your maximum potential.

4

If You Think You Can't— You're Right

In the last chapter, I explained how beliefs are formed. A brief review is:

- Information is taken in through touch, sight, smell, taste and hearing.
- The information is processed and beliefs are developed.
- Beliefs differ greatly in intensity, based on the strength of the experience.
- Similar beliefs tend to cluster together.
- Clusters tend to have a positive value, a negative value or indifference—based on the overall total experiences related to that cluster.

Millions of messages are received each day through the five senses. As each series of messages hits the hard drive of your subconscious, the belief statements cluster around the incoming data and formulate a response, either positive, negative, or indifferent. Let's reconsider the "dog" example in Chapter 3 and create a new scenario. Remember that much of this happens without any conscious thought.

I see a dog. It is a Black Labrador.

My response:

Look at that dog. It is just like my grandmother's dog, Alf. (Positive, great intensity). *Belief: Black Labs are great dogs.*

He's running loose; maybe I should be careful (negative). *Belief: Wild dogs are dangerous.*

He has tags, looks okay (positive). *Belief: Dogs with tags are probably tame.*

As all the beliefs gather together and submit their information, a final conclusion is derived and I move into action. I kneel down and whistle, trying to get the dog to come to me so I can pet him. If he does, the response reinforces my beliefs, which become even stronger. If he responds instead with a growl, the new data may alter my belief about black Labs. You can apply this same process to any scenario, be it dogs, cars, sports, men, women . . . whatever.

Guess what? Oh no! Your beliefs may not be true!

Yes, your beliefs are the result of your experiences, but are they true? We tend to think they are true because they happened to us and, *based on my experience,* they are true. But, are they true compared to all the data available? I have found that many of our beliefs are not true. A group of experts could sit around a table and we both know that they would not all agree on what is and isn't true. Even those involved in research projects tend to disagree on the conclusions drawn from the research.

Activity 5

Listed below are several quotes from famous people in history. These quotes (or belief statements) may or may not be true. What do you think? Circle your answer. Could you **possibly disagree** with people of this stature? Note that I have added my personal comments in italics.

- We don't know a millionth of one percent
  about anything.   True False

    Speak for yourself, Thomas Edison.

- Nothing in life is to be feared;
  it is only to be understood.   True False

    If you're going to try to understand Mt. Everest by climbing it, you had better be afraid, Marie Curie.

- There is only one happiness in life,
  to love and be loved. True False

  *I don't know about that, George Sand. I get a lot of happiness when
  I hit a long straight 300 yard drive down the middle of the fairway,
  but love is good, too.*

- An investment in knowledge pays
  the best interest. True False

  *Actually, Mr. Ben Franklin, I've done pretty well in the stock
  market.*

- If the world should blow itself up, the last audible voice
  would be that of an expert saying that it can't be done. True False

  Peter Ustinov, I agree with you on that one!

- We tend to get what we expect. True False

  Thank you, Norman Vincent Peale, preach it!

- Whether you think you can or can't, you are right! True False

  *If you think you can't, you are right. If you think you can, you may
  or may not be right.*

Did you agree with the famous people? Did you agree with me? Our
beliefs are different, which means that what we believe to be true and
false is different from what others believe.

Think about this: I've invested the past four chapters telling you
something you already know—we are all different.

Listen to this quote from Charles Duell, the Director of the U.S.
Patent Office:

"Everything that can be invented, has been invented."

Unbelievably, this statement was made in the year 1899. Now consider
Lee De Forest and his famous opinion from 1926:

"Theoretically and technically, television may be feasible. Commer-
cially and financially, I consider it an impossibility—a development on
which we need waste little time or dreaming."

I'll bet he was an expert in his day. We are surrounded by people who tell
us "it can't be done" and we believe them! If you believe it can't be done,
you are right. Here are some other famous can'ts:

- Man will never fly.
- No one can run the mile in under 4:00 minutes.

At the time of this writing, the world record for the men's mile is a stunning 3:44.39 minutes—a full 16 seconds under that which could not be done.

People dared to challenge accepted beliefs and found them to be false. The mile can be and is run in under four minutes; air travel has dramatically decreased the size of the world.

Fact: We believe things about ourselves and others that, when put to the test, are not true.

Mt. Everest has laid out a challenge to women and men throughout the world: "Climb me." Each year, two questions surround the mountain:

- Who will live?
- Who will die?

All who have attempted the ascent to the peak have believed that they were capable and would make the summit. Some did, some didn't. On every ascent, Everest challenges their beliefs and their abilities. Some of the best climbers in the world have died, while some amateur climbers have survived. Each year teams go to the mountain. Some walk away thankful for their lives, vowing never to return. Some are buried on the mountain. Some fail and return again and again. Some succeed, but all believed initially that they could conquer the highest mountain in the world.

If I ascended to the peak of Everest once, I may believe I can conquer the mountain anytime I choose. The next time, there might be obstacles that were not present on the first climb, causing failure. Conquering the ominous mountain once is not proof that it will bow again, as many climbers have discovered.

When facing a challenge, our belief system tells us "we can" or "we can't." We act based on that belief system. If we believe we can, we may try. If we believe we can't, we never will.

If you believe you can't, you are right!

Why? Because you will not try. If you do not try, you will never know how much you could have achieved. You will never know the thrill of accomplishment or the satisfaction of knowing that you gave it your best shot. If you believe you can't, you should put that belief to the test.

Here's an interesting comment from Theodore Roosevelt that is apropos to this idea:

> The credit belongs to those who are actually in the arena, who strive valiantly; who know the great enthusiasms, the great devotions, and spend themselves in a worthy cause; who, at the best know the triumph of high achievement and who, at the worst, if they fail, fail while daring greatly, so that their place shall never be with those cold and timid souls who know neither victory nor defeat.

If you believe you can't, you should try. You must put the belief to the test or you will never know if it is just a limiting belief—holding you back, dooming you to mediocrity.

If you think you can—Try! Go for it! Make sure you ensure your personal safety if the act you desire to do is potentially life threatening. You may prove that the impossible is really possible. You will get farther in life by trying than you will by not trying.

My point is that you cannot automatically accept your belief system as true. The experience of living will test your beliefs, gradually refining and purifying their validity. Unfortunately, many men and women go through life unwilling to try new things, unwilling to stretch themselves into new areas, never challenging their beliefs, never realizing that they are so much more than they ever thought they would be—never realizing their potential.

Remember, you are far more than you think you are!

Activity 6

1. List things you believe you can never do. _____

_____

_____

_____

_____

   a. Who told you, or why do you believe you can't do it?

   b. Are you sure you are right?

   c. If you don't try, how will you know?

2. List things you've dreamed of doing. _____

_____

_____

_____

_____

    a. Are they possible? Don't say no!
    b. Will you try?

3. At your job, if you have one, what is your weekly wage? $_____
    a. Is that what you are really worth?
    b. Could you ever believe you should be paid ten times that much?
      One hundred?

Entrepreneurs all over the world are earning more than they ever dreamed possible because they tried. They had a dream of having their own business, stepped out and found an ability to succeed, unknown to them beforehand. If you think you can't, you are right because you will never try.

If you devote your energy to being the best that you can be, then you will try and you will go far beyond your wildest dreams, because you are significantly greater than you think you are. YOU can win. The greatest limitations you have are the beliefs in your head that say "I can't." Other great men and women have overcome these beliefs, such as the famous painter, Pablo Picasso, who said: "I am always doing that which I cannot do, in order that I may learn how to do it."

5

Is There a Champion Within?

Personal growth and development is a lifelong process. The first step in that process is an accurate understanding of yourself. My research has validated the *why* of your actions, *why* you will move from point A to point B. This chapter defines basic concepts you need to understand—concepts incorporated into a process that will assist you in achieving your maximum potential.

Dr. David Warburton, founder and president of ARISE (Associated Researchers in the Science of Enjoyment), associated with the University of Reading in the United Kingdom, was an important contributor to this chapter.

There are four terms you will need to know and remember as you read further:

- The Real Self
- The Ideal Self
- Self-Efficacy
- Self-Esteem

According to Dr. Warburton, the *Real Self* is the one you sense, whether or not your self-perceptions are accurate or shared by others. The *Ideal Self* embodies those aspects you would like to possess.

Note that your Real Self, the one you sense, may or may not be true. In other words, you may not know *you* as well as you should. My goal is to help you better understand yourself and increase your appreciation of your own unique design.

Dr. Warburton also states that the discrepancy between the Real Self and the Ideal Self results in an internal conflict, and "people strive to make the Real Self more like the Ideal Self, in order to relieve anxiety."

As you envision your Ideal Self, you will be motivated to move in that direction, seeking out the activities, places, and people necessary to advance you toward the ideal. The Ideal Self, or the "what you would like to be" self is "influenced by feedback from other people and information you have absorbed (and believed) from other sources, like the media."

A picture of your two selves might look like this:

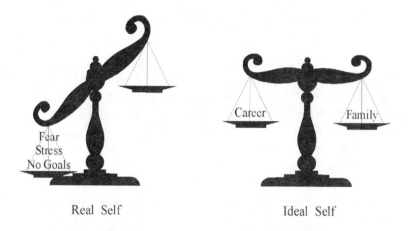

Real Self   Ideal Self

Obviously, these two images are vastly different, which means you are probably experiencing internal conflict. Consequently, achieving the Ideal Self may be a totally unrealistic expectation, even if you think you can. The result of continually coming up short of an Ideal Self is low self-esteem and a low valuing of your life and purpose. Your Ideal Self must be realistic and achievable. A realistic Ideal Self emanates from a true picture of your Real Self. If you **know** your Real Self, **understand** your Real Self, and **value** your Real Self, then the effect will be positive as you recreate and progress toward an **achievable** Ideal Self.

Our two pictures will then look like this:

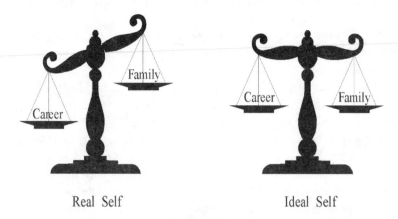

Real Self   Ideal Self

Years of research have led me to agree with Dr. Warburton:

> Psychologically healthy individuals have a close enough fit between their Ideal and Real selves to feel good about themselves, their activities, and have a high self-esteem.

Conversely,

> Those whose Ideal Self is unrealistic and much different from their Real Self, go through life with low self-esteem and suffer from the tyranny of the "should," the constant anxious feeling that they should be doing things differently or better than they currently do.

Overly high self expectations (Ideal Self) will actually hurt your progress. As you continually fall significantly short of your ideal, the result will be lowered self-esteem and self-efficacy. A truer image of who you are (Real Self) and a realistic expectation of who you can become will result in a greater personal valuing of life, higher self-esteem and improved self-efficacy.

Which takes us to the definition of two more terms:

Self-Efficacy is a very strong internal drive that believes "I CAN DO IT" when attempting to achieve a goal. If you believe you can accomplish certain tasks, you are said to have a high self-efficacy about the task. If you believe you cannot accomplish a certain task, you are said to have a low self-efficacy about it. In other words, even after failure you will attempt again because everything in you says you can do it! Most entrepreneurs have a strong self-efficacy—they see and do things others cannot see and they are often criticized for their dedication to the project which they believe they can do.

Self-Esteem is a feeling of self worth. Simply stated, if you feel good about yourself, who you are, and what you are becoming, you will live a happier life.

Self-efficacy and self-esteem have a cause and effect cycle relationship. Increased self-esteem leads to increased self-efficacy. Decreased self-esteem leads to decreased self-efficacy.

Finding the champion that is within each of us requires certain things. When you are in an environment that values who you are, you develop a healthy self-esteem. This leads to high self-efficacy. Believing you can achieve, you then put forth more effort. You try harder. Your increased effort in pursuit of your goal results in success. You success is often recognized by others. The recognition of your successes leads to even higher self-esteem, and the cycle continues.

Personal development is a process. You move toward your maximum potential or you zero out. You are in the process of positively building your self-esteem and your self-efficacy, or you are in the negative process of destroying your self-esteem and self-efficacy. That negative process could be called the Zero Cycle. It is the gradual destruction of who you are, your Real Self. When you operate in an environment that does not value you—an environment that discourages or hinders your personal growth and development—you will experience low self-esteem, which leads directly to low self-efficacy.

When you believe (through feedback and experiences) that you cannot achieve a desired goal, you will exert little or no effort toward achieving it. As soon as a few obstacles arise, you will probably give up on it. Little or no effort results in minimal success, if any. You will not be positively recognized for failure; you may even be condemned or disciplined, which results in even lower self-esteem.

Here are just a few of the benefits of moving toward the high self-esteem and self-efficacy experiences: fewer sleepless nights, no ulcer problems, you are less likely to use drugs, and it is easier not to succumb to pressure to conform. You are just a happier person all the way around. Don't you think it is worth it?

Warning! Warning! No longer can you just "put up with your job." The continual battering of your self-esteem gradually wears you down. You are not designed to be devalued. You are designed to be a valued, significant person. We have all seen talented people destroyed by careers that paid high wages, but did not build their self-esteem. That is a high price to pay. I have counseled people to leave successful careers that were destroying them and start their own businesses, and I have seen them achieve heights they never thought possible. Honoring that self within is a must—not an option!

We have talked about Real Self, Ideal Self, self-esteem, and self-efficacy. Beyond the Ideal Self is a level of achievement and growth that we will call the Potential Self. This is all you were meant to be. Your Potential Self far exceeds anything you could ever imagine. By moving along with a championship attitude you will go past your Ideal Self and move into areas of unparalleled richness. To move you toward your Potential Self, I will give you a key understanding of your Real Self and what impels you to action. With a truer self-awareness, you can then analyze your current environment, make the appropriate changes necessary, and plot a course to an achievable Ideal Self.

6

The Real Self: A Truer Picture

We have defined the Real Self as the one you sense, your self-perception, regardless of whether or not your perceptions are accurate or shared by others. My objective now is to give you a truer picture of your Real Self and what motivates you to action. Understanding your motivations, you will be able to take charge of your life and the decisions you make will result in higher self-esteem and a more fulfilling life.

With the many assessments in the marketplace today it is difficult to choose one that can really give you a clear picture of "who you are." Many people, maybe even yourself, have been excited to learn about the differences between people, only to find that you were labeled, pigeon-holed, and stereotyped—most of which is nothing more than "psycho-babble." It is extremely important to have the assessments validated for what they are measuring. Remember,

"'Tis not knowing much, but what is useful, that makes a wise man."
Thomas Fuller, M.D.

You are intricate and complex. To over-simplify who you are takes away from your individualism and uniqueness. In my life-long effort to understand people, I have adhered to the following guidelines:

Integrity: I will walk slowly into the understanding of the person, saying only what I can validate through research.

Caution: With every step, I will ask if it is a step that should be taken and if it will help people. After taking the step, I look back and review it, asking, "Can we say that and can we defend it?"

Self-Esteem: The goal of all my behavioral writing and research is to build your self-esteem, to help you become the champion you were meant to be.

Synergy: Even though I separate the person into components that I can understand individually, I am awed by the wonderful synergy as the parts come together and interact, producing an effect that can never be measured.

Personality: The personality is the sum total of each of the parts of the Real Self. No instrument exists that can even come close to assessing the uniqueness of your personality. Therefore, I use the term "personality" very cautiously.

Based on the above guidelines I have adopted, the following can be stated:

• I know what I know.

• I know what I know is true.

• If I don't know, I will tell you that I don't know, and then I will speculate.

• After I speculate, I will find a way to validate.

• After I validate, I will know more than I knew.

As we discuss the components of your Real Self, your awareness should increase in three areas:

1. An appreciation of the complexity and uniqueness of each individual person.

2. Without some type of testing we lack words to articulate who we really are.

3. The necessity of a cautious, well-validated approach when attempting to understand a complex being such as yourself.

I believe most psychologists and theologians would agree that you are made up of three overall interwoven elements: body, soul, and spirit.

- Body: your physical self

- Soul: your total self (personality)

- Spirit: the life-giving force (often argued to be the same as the soul.)

The focus of our analysis is the soul, often referred to as the seat of a person's desires, emotions, and passions. Your soul (total self) expresses its uniqueness through your body (physical self) in speech and actions. Your body is the vehicle for the expression of your soul as well as the window to your soul. The essence of who you are cannot be seen unless it is expressed through your words and actions. If, deep inside, you want to be an artist, would you not express that desire through painting or sculpture? You take action through your body to express and fulfill the desires of your soul. If you happened to see an artist's exhibit, you value it as the artist's impressions come through your senses to your soul. Your body supplies your soul with information. Your artistic soul values the impressions given by your body and enjoys a memorable experience.

I know a man who has an incredible natural ability to make money. His sense of investment and return is uncanny. His speech and actions express his soul. He started out as a salesperson for an eyeglass frame company; through perseverance he is now one of the most respected men in the optical industry in the United States. To hear him speak for five minutes is like getting a degree in economics. The impressions his soul receives from his body are all translated into investment and return, both in time and money. His passion is to produce for the consumer. He is one of those people who could lose all of his material possessions and gain them back, with more, within one year—and love the challenge!

I referred to the soul as your "total self, your personality." Your Real Self is comprised of several distinct parts, each interacting and producing a single you—an active in-process person—never to be duplicated.

Here are a few facts and opinions:

Fact 1:	Your Real Self is made up of several distinct parts, some of which can be measured.
Fact 2:	We know and can identify some of the parts.
Opinion 1:	There may be parts that we are not aware of.
Fact 3:	All of the individual unique parts interact with each other in varying intensities, forming the total self, your personality (soul).
Opinion 2:	If I were able to identify and measure each aspect of your Real Self, the interaction and the marriage of all the parts would be impossible to measure.
Fact 4:	Even though my evidence suggests that Opinion 2 is probably true, I will still cautiously attempt to understand each of the parts of the Real Self and their interaction.

It would take several lifetimes to collect the information and validate it to comprehensively explain your total self. To print it would require more pages than any library in the world could contain. Can we possibly identify and explain all of the varying interactions of the components of your personality? We're talking billions of possibilities.

Let's identify several components of your Real Self, remembering that they all interact to form a unique you. I'll italicize and boldface the areas that can be measured effectively.

Genetics/Heredity: How much of you is from Mom and Dad? We know that many physical traits are passed down, but what about elements in the non-physical realm? We all have heard the statement "she comes from good stock." Are traits from the soul of the parents passed to the child?

Behavior: Behavior is the *how* of your actions, your methodology of action, your *modus operandi*. Some people are extroverted while others are introverted; some bold and daring, while others are relaxed and cautious. Your behavior is neutral, neither good nor bad.

Intelligence: Intelligence is the ability to learn or understand. The IQ test is a common tool for measuring intelligence. My personal opinion is that the definition of intelligence promoted by the IQ test is too narrow.

Skills: Skills you have learned can be measured simply by having you perform them and comparing you to an accepted standard.

Life and Work Experience: A science fiction television character said, "We are the sum total of all our experiences." As stated in an earlier chapter, our experiences continually impact our belief system, but can we measure the effect of life experiences on the Real Self? Probably not.

Education and Training: We know education and training have an effect on your Real Self. We can list your degrees and the seminars you have attended, but two questions must be asked to measure your education and training: (1) What did you learn? and (2) How did you apply it?

Purpose and Direction in Life: What do you believe? Not what do you say you believe—but, what do you really believe? Can beliefs be measured? Yes.

Attitudes? Yes, I am going to change your definition of this word. Your attitudes explain WHY you do what you do in life and impel you to act. We can measure your attitudes. They are not good or bad—they are you. Your beliefs and attitudes give you purpose and direction in life.

The above components interact with each other in varying degrees, forming a complex, potentially wonderful, actively developing person—YOU.

There are several more components that have not been identified, such as your mind and will. Are you getting a picture of how complex and unique you are? I hope so. That's why I proceed with extreme caution as I attempt to understand you and help you understand and appreciate yourself and others.

The word "attitude" was introduced earlier. You've probably been told that you have either a great attitude or a bad attitude. Research dating as far back as the early 1900s with Edward Spranger identified six attitudes with which we view the world. These attitudes impel you to action, determining how and what you value in life. The fulfillment of these attitudes results in your fulfillment in life. These attitudes dictate why you do what you do.

Your attitudes are part of your Real Self, one part of you I have measured and validated. By understanding your personal attitudes and the attitudes of others, you will put yourself in the driver's seat of your life, having the knowledge and ability to make decisions that will increase your enjoyment of life.

After an overall view of the complex task of self understanding and appreciation, it is time to focus on one distinct area of your Real Self. Your attitudes, the reason *why* you act, may be the most powerful component of your Real Self. The intensity of your attitudes has an incredible effect on the other components of your Real Self. Your attitudes impel the passion that drives your actions. If you can understand why you act, you can apply this knowledge to order your world and achieve a new satisfaction and value of life.

You will find as you proceed in understanding your attitudes that I have validated an aspect of you that you did not know previously and my validation is immensely powerful in assisting you to achieve satisfaction and meaning in life. Your attitudes are an integral part of this positive cycle, getting you on the fast track to your Ideal Self and your Potential Self. Understanding your attitudes can be the most important material available to help you become all you can be. Attitudes—the *why* of your Real Self.

7

You've Got Attitude— What is It?

Your attitudes drive your actions, moving you from your Real Self to your Potential Self. They are the reasons *why* you act.

In review of past chapters, let us look at the argument for proper emphasis on the uniqueness of the individual. When we deal with issues of self-esteem and self-efficacy, we do not have the liberty to say whatever we want. Understanding human behavior would be very easy if we were all alike. Then, when one truth was validated, it could apply to every living person. For example, the field of sales has several universal methods for answering objections. If the buyer presents a certain objection, sales people are trained to answer it one way, and that way is supposed to work with every buyer. I think the one I dislike the most is called "Feel, Felt, Found." Here's how it is used: the sales person receives an objection from the buyer and responds like this: "I know how you *feel*, I *felt* the same way, but here's what I *found. . . .*"

This universal approach is supposed to work every time. It doesn't. I once read an article in the paper about a salesperson who continued to pursue the close until the potential customer physically attacked him! Legal charges ensued and when asked why he wouldn't stop selling, the salesperson responded, "My boss told me that when a person says 'no' it just means he wants more information!" That's a nice universal "truth," but sometimes NO means NO.

In most conversations, casual or business, one hears sweeping generalizations made with very little thought supporting the statements. Often they are accepted as fact and decisions are made that do not build a

41

person's self-esteem. How many times have you heard someone say, "All men do that. It's a man thing."

Now there are books published that say men are from one planet and women are from another. Think about that for a second. If men are from one planet and women from another, how can we possibly understand each other? We're doomed from the beginning. We can't succeed. If that were the case, we should each go back to our own planet and try to live out our lives. No thank you.

The fact is this. In terms of behavior, men and women are very similar. We *can* understand, appreciate, and communicate effectively with one another. Here are a few more of those "truths":

- Boys and girls are normal if they can sit quietly in school and stay on task.
- Everyone should get a college education.
- There is a perfect golf swing.
- If you are loyal to your company and work hard, you will be rewarded.

With minimal effort I could list hundreds more. We hear them every day and we judge others by these supposed universal truths. But, how do they get to be universal?

The process is relatively simple and unsophisticated:

I have an experience → I believe it to be true → I believe it to be universally true for all humanity.

I believe it to be universally true for *all* humanity because *I experienced it.* That is the sum total of my "universal" validation. I experienced it and therefore it must be true for everyone. Most "universals" only hold true for a very small percentage of the population because we are *all* different.

Here's a true personal example to illustrate the danger of the "universal truth." Recently I purchased a car. I called a dealer friend in Iowa and told him that I wanted a Lincoln Continental. He told me what he had, we negotiated a price, and I sent him a check. Sight unseen, a driver was hired to bring my new car from Iowa to Scottsdale, Arizona. I have been enjoying it ever since. Would you buy a car the same way I did?

Most people would not buy a car sight unseen, from a dealer in another state, and hire a person to deliver it. But, suppose that *I* believe everyone in the world buys cars the way I do. Taking that a step further, let's suppose I am also the owner of a car dealership and I have that belief. Here is the kind of experience you will have when you want to buy a car from me:

- I do not have a showroom. Why do you need to see the car?
- No one is allowed to test drive a car. Why do you need to?
- We carry no inventory. You've seen the cars on the road or TV.
- Pick out the car you want based on the features you want. We'll order it on the computer and have someone drive it here from the factory.
- Give me your check, up front.
- When would you like delivery?

Would you buy a car from me? I don't think so. My "universal truth" is not universal. That truth is limited to a very few.

It is easy to make generalizations based on limited experience, but most of these, upon closer examination, are not universal at all. They are true for some people, but not all. Look at these: Do blondes really have more fun? If you work hard and are loyal, will you be rewarded in the modern corporation? Is there a perfect golf swing?

"Universal truths" become dangerous when we hold them out as the standard and measure others against them. It is a travesty to judge someone against a standard that is simply not true. I am continually amazed at the many false statements made in seminars and in books by educated people. Many are based only on personal observation and opinion.

In the study of human behavior and motivation, researchers must maintain an open and questioning mind. We are dealing with self-esteem, and our process of moving from the specific to the universal should be immersed in caution, similar to the following:

I experience something → I believe it to be true to this situation → I speculate as to whether it might be a universal truth → I remain open minded to experiences which may contradict the one I just had.

At this time, reviewing the Real Self and the Ideal Self is appropriate:

The Real Self is a unique combination of genetics, heredity, skills, experience, education, training, values, beliefs, attitudes, and behavior. These interact creating the total, unique you. Each of these components is completely different in each person and the "working together" of the components differs greatly from person to person. The Ideal Self will grow out of a solid concrete foundation if you have an accurate awareness of your Real Self. We know that a significant difference between the Real and Ideal leads to stress and poor self-esteem. Therefore, it is important to provide you with accurate, validated information about your Real Self that puts you in control and allows you to move toward your Ideal Self.

To achieve your maximum potential (Potential Self), you must be on a positive course. Note:

> If you are in an environment where you are valued, you will have high self-esteem → With healthy self-esteem, you will begin to believe that you can achieve a goal (self-efficacy) → Self-esteem and self-efficacy will lead you to increased effort, determination, and persistence toward your goals → Your success will lead to recognition → Recognition leads to increased self-esteem, self-efficacy, and even greater effort.

Life is an active process. Relationships are active. We have all met many people who are unhappy with their lives and careers, who are "just putting up with it." It's more than that! You are gradually, systematically destroying who you are! You are like the frog in the pot of water—getting boiled to death without realizing that the water is gradually getting hotter. The price is too high and you have to get on a positive cycle—now! Today! Your value and potential contribution to humanity are too great to allow yourself to waste away. Make sure you are on a positive course and if not, begin to make changes *today*!

As you get more information on your Real Self, you will begin to value who you are and may even decide to make some immediate changes in your environment. Your value of your Real Self will then lead you to re-define your Ideal Self and believe that you can achieve it. With a conscious act of will, you can then move toward your Ideal Self, resulting in increased self-esteem. A continuous repetition of this process will lead you to achieve more than you ever dreamed possible. Remember—a journey of one thousand miles begins with a single step.

You can only become the best you can be by first knowing who you are.

Now, back to attitudes and how to help you to understand the attitudes that motivate you. These attitudes are universal in the sense that my international research indicates that these world views are true. Remember, we are only looking at one aspect of your Real Self. The attitudes are hierarchical within you and the top two will move you to action. You can increase the value of your life by making sure that your career and social environments are consistent with your attitudes. When you are in an environment that is consistent with your attitudes, you will feel valued and begin to believe that you can achieve.

The understanding of these attitudes has revolutionalized my own life and career. The thousands of people trained on attitudes worldwide have experienced tremendous personal growth as they learned that they are very special as individuals. With an increased understanding of their Real Selves, many of them have turned a mess into a masterpiece.

- I give you permission to become all you can be.
- I give you permission to be the president of your life and call the shots.
- I give you permission to define success in your terms.

My desire is that you enjoy a new life with new values, and when you are in the golden years, you can look back with satisfaction and say, "What a journey! What a ride!" Imagine the satisfaction of knowing you have fulfilled your destiny. In the words of Louis L'Amour:

Knowledge is like money: to be of value it must circulate, and in circulating it can increase in quantity and, hopefully, in value.

8

Let's Identify an Attitude

Picture six individuals at an art auction, viewing "Starry Night" painted by Vincent Van Gogh. Each of the six has the ability to invest the millions of dollars necessary to own the work. Each has a completely different reason for wanting to own the painting. By going inside the mind of each one of these people, you will see the reason *why* they act, which comes from their specific "attitude."

Fred: That painting will increase in value over the next several years. The return I will get is worth the investment of money. (**Utilitarian Attitude**)

Louise: Works of this magnitude should be shared with everyone, not kept in a private collection. I will purchase this work and place it in a museum so that all can enjoy its greatness. (**Social Attitude**)

Joanne: Notice the circles moving from the moon. When was this painted? Why did Van Gogh paint the circles that way? I think I read that he might have had a problem with eyesight. I want to learn all I can about this painting after I buy it. (**Theoretical Attitude**)

Hannah: I must own this painting. It is a significant work of art. My collection will be considered one of the most prized in the world with the addition of this work. (**Individual-istic Attitude**)

Bernard: What a beautiful work of art. It speaks to me of the greatness of man. Van Gogh was at the peak of his artistic expression. I want to own it and design an exquisite display in my living room. Look at the colors and the brush strokes. The painting seems to come alive as I observe it; it speaks to me. (**Aesthetic Attitude**)

John: "Starry Night" reminds me of the divine in life. The moon and the stars speak of a grand design, causing us to look up and achieve all we can achieve. The moon and stars dance together in a unity of expression, compelling us to move beyond ourselves and reach out to something or someone bigger than ourselves; a unifying force that holds it all together. I will buy this painting because it speaks to me of things larger than life. (**Traditional Attitude**)

All six people in the room are interested in the painting. All are interested in the painting for different reasons. Each one views the painting through different eyes — **a different attitude**.

Looking at the six attitudes as shown above, we can put the same six individuals in a career counseling session to plan their future. Each is asked the question, "What type of career or vocation would really motivate you and cause you to be your best?" Look at their responses in relation to their particular attitude.

Fred: I definitely want to be a businessman, but not necessarily in a corporation. I prefer more of an upstart business or maybe sales; something where the return of money for my time would be relatively quick. I might be willing to invest several years in college if it resulted in a job that would pay me an income commensurate with the time invested, like maybe six figures. (**Utilitarian Attitude**)

Louise: I want to be involved in some type of work that really helps people. I think I am going to join the Peace Corps or maybe become a nurse or social worker. We have a responsibility to humanity, to help people become better. It's really more of a mission than a career. (**Social Attitude**)

Joanne: I can't wait to get to college. There is so much that I do not know, and the wealth of wisdom and knowledge available is incredible. I think I would enjoy a career as a

	researcher or historian; a career where I could continue to learn. **(Theoretical Attitude)**
Hannah:	I believe that I have great leadership qualities, and I want a career that allows me to lead people. I want to be the head of a corporation or maybe go into one of the military academies. Hey, has there ever been a woman five star general? I could be the President of the United States. Cool! **(Individualistic Attitude)**
Bernard:	I may not go to college. I want to find a place where I can develop my artistic abilities. Several people have looked at my paintings and my photography and said that I have talent. I've actually sold a few paintings. I don't really like to sell them, but it does pay a few bills. I've also thought about working in the National Parks. I really enjoy the beauty of nature and want to work to help protect and preserve it. **(Aesthetic Attitude)**
John:	I want to change the world. I want my life to count for something. I'm currently involved in my local political party. We're making a difference. I may go to college, get my degree, and then get involved in politics. Forces are at work shaping humanity for the next century. I want to be on the cutting edge, shaping the future. I have ideas for change that I know will work. **(Traditional Attitude)**

Each person has an **attitude**. The following statement is one that I use in my seminars:

All people are motivated, but people do things for their reasons, not yours.

It is imperative that we realize that people are different. Each of the six people can be motivated to action but the motivation is different. If we held out high wages to all six, only a few would be motivated. All people want high wages in life, right? Wrong! People want what they want and if you give them something other than what they want, they will either not care or be negative toward your offer. Let me provide you with a true example.

Phil was the top salesperson at an auto dealership. He made a very good living in sales and was consistently on the leader board. His office walls were laden with his monthly plaques for being the top salesperson, as well as several awards he had won in the community. He was known in several states as one of the top auto salespersons.

Despite all this, Phil was unhappy. He felt he wasn't getting the recognition he deserved. He had the biggest office but felt that the dealership should let him drive, as his demo, one of the luxury cars. He wanted his own advertising in the newspaper with his picture featured. The general sales manager realized after a training session in attitudes that Phil liked the amount of money he was making but the motivator for his success was position; he wanted to be known and seen as the top salesperson he was. The general sales manager immediately provided him with the keys to a brand new luxury car as his demo. The luxury car gave him the status that he believed he had earned.

I saw Phil shortly after that, tooling around in his new demo. He rolled down the window and with a big grin on his face, said, "Thanks for training them on that attitudes stuff. This is the kind of car that the Number One Man deserves!"

An attitude is a worldview. It is a way of looking at and valuing life; a mindset; a paradigm of thought and a filter through which we view the world.

In studying the history of attitudes, it is necessary to look at the work of Edward Spranger, a German psychologist, teacher, and philosopher who published a book in 1928 entitled *Types of Men*. In this work, he identified the six attitudes, or windows, through which we observe the world. He believed, although it was not validated at that time, that these six attitudes were universally true.

The attitudes form a hierarchy (strongest to weakest) within you. The top two are the dominant attitudes which drive you to action and determine your valuation of life. The attitudes defined by Spranger are not a set of clothing—put on in the morning and taken off at night—but are an integral part of your Real Self.

I have taken the writings of Edward Spranger and developed and validated an attitudes assessment program called "Personal Interests, Attitudes, and Values." The longer I work with Spranger's material, the more powerful it seems to become. Your attitudes relate to your overall satisfaction and valuation of life. If you are not fulfilling the passions within you, you will find little satisfaction in life.

Your attitudes are active, consisting of strong desires and feelings which I call passions. When you are engaged in an activity or discussion that is in line with your attitudes, you will be excited and enthusiastic about it. If your career is an extension of your attitudes, you will love getting up in the morning and going into action. If your career runs counter to your attitudes, you will find little or no satisfaction in your job.

Research shows that almost 40 percent of executives would select a different career if they could replace their income level. Why would you or anyone intentionally choose to be dissatisfied? If you know what drives your actions, then you can make choices that will lead to satisfaction in life.

Where do the attitudes come from? The answer to this question is speculative. Essentially, three fields of thought have been promoted by the three people who have invested the most time into this subject. Edward Spranger, Gordon Allport, and myself.

View 1: Become What You Are

Spranger believed that your attitudes are predetermined. You are born with an attitude seed that eventually reveals itself (age 16–18) and you will become what you were intended to become.

Spranger's view places little value on life experience, skills, education, and training. Your attitudes are predetermined. Who predetermined them? God? Nature? Spranger has no answer. I reject this view because I believe strongly that your life experiences have an incredible impact on the development of your attitudes and your personality.

View 2: Be All That You Can Be

This view, espoused by psychologist Gordon Allport, says that inside you there is an active "self" constantly striving to achieve its maximum potential. The "self" is motivated by the environment, not genetics or heredity.

Allport's error is the opposite of Spranger's. Life experience is emphasized as the driving force in your development. Little or no emphasis is placed on the genetic element.

View 3: The Dance

I believe that genetics and life experience "dance together" to form YOU. I cannot discount genetics and heredity, nor do I want to underestimate the effect of the billions of life experiences which you have had. We may be predetermined to some degree. Some people may be "designed" to be businesspersons, artists, or politicians. Nature and nurture dance together to develop and form YOU. Let me speculate on the the process which formulates your attitudes:

- You have experiences.
- Multiple experiences lead to beliefs of varying intensities.
- Similar beliefs tend to cluster together.
- The clustering together of beliefs, combined with a possible genetic element, lead to a . . .
- Hierarchy of attitudes.

Think of it this way: one hears, observes, and experiences a thing, it leads to a belief, and the more you hear, observe, and experience, the more you create a cluster of beliefs. As in the Circle Graph earlier in the book, after the cluster is formed you will think and evaluate in a positive or negative manner, which then leads to an attitude, either positive or negative. Your way of valuing (positive) or judging (negative) leads to a need, and then an action, and the behavior is used to satisfy.

Your attitudes are hierarchical and as I've said before, the top two are the dominant ones, which impel you to action. Normally when we hear the word "attitude," we hear it in the context of having a good one or a bad one. Your attitudes, as I use the term, are not good or bad. They are the way you view the world.

I am constantly amazed at how others view the world differently than I do. My natural inclination is to call all of them wrong, but I have learned to find a beauty in their different perspectives. I now enjoy conversing with others and seeing the world through their eyes. They can have the same experience as I and walk away with a completely different perspective and valuation of the experience. Instead of judging people as wrong, I now find myself asking many more questions and listening intently to the answers. Daily I learn more and more about people.

Your attitudes are a significant portion of your Real Self. They drive your actions. If you are in an environment where you fulfill the passions of your dominant attitudes, you will feel valued (self-esteem). If your passions are being fulfilled, you will believe that you can achieve (self-efficacy) and will supply increased effort, determination, and persistence. With your successes, you will gain recognition, which will lead to greater self-esteem. You are well on your way to becoming more than you ever dreamed possible.

If your attitudes are not being met, you will not feel valued and will find yourself gradually losing your self-esteem and your self-efficacy. You will not believe that you can achieve. Your job becomes just a job—a paycheck—nothing more. Understanding your attitudes is a significant step.

Following is a list of the six attitudes. Look at the explanations of each and remember that the two dominant attitudes drive your actions and interactions.

Theoretical Attitude:	A passion to know, seek out, understand, and systematize the truth.
Utilitarian Attitude:	A passion to gain a return on all investments involving time, money, and resources.
Aesthetic Attitude:	A passion to enjoy and experience my impressions of the world around me and allow them to mold me into all I can be.
Individualistic Attitude:	A drive to control your own destiny. A passion to lead.
Social Attitude:	A passion to invest myself, my time, and my resources into helping others achieve their potential.
Traditional Attitude:	A passion to find and pursue the highest meaning in life, in the divine, and in the ideal.

Did any one of these sound a lot like you? Which one? Put a mark next to it. You will be doing simple assessments in the following chapters to identify the hierarchy of your attitudes. When you know your attitudes, your choices and decisions will enhance your valuation of life. For example, if you know that you have a Social Attitude, you can search out activities and careers that allow you to help others. In doing so, you will gain tremendous personal satisfaction (self-esteem). By assisting you in understanding the part of your Real Self that contains your attitudes, I place you in a position that will allow you to value who you are. If you value who you are, you will make sure that you are in an environment where you can grow and reach your Potential Self. I know, based on my research, that if you are in a career or activity that is in line with your attitudes, you will feel more valued and satisfied with life. If you are in an activity or job that is not in line with your attitudes . . . well, I have seen that happen and that's why this book is being written.

In each of the following chapters, I explain one of the attitudes and provide you with an opportunity to rate yourself with regard to that attitude. By the end we will be able to determine your top two attitudes. Several processes will be outlined allowing you to examine the effect of your attitudes on your career, communications, and relationships.

As you approach an understanding of the attitudes, remember that no one attitude is better than another. Each is unique and adds value to the world. If passions are met on the job, you'll feel differently than if they are not, and my goal is to help you understand your motivations and then apply this knowledge to your life.

9

What are Your Top Two Attitudes?

On the following pages you are going to do exercises with each of the six attitudes to help you discover your top two attitudes. We can start off with the Theoretical Attitude. If you have a strong Theoretical Attitude, you have a desire to know and to learn. Life is a constant education. You are always learning and growing. Your attitude is a powerful part of your Real Self. It is driven to know, learn, systematize, categorize, and analyze. You will find fulfillment in life and value life as you are able to learn and know. You will experience dissatisfaction if you cannot seek out, discover, and learn.

Listed on the next page are ten statements describing the Theoretical Attitude. Score each statement according to the 5–1 scale shown below. At the end of the ten statements you will total your score. Do this exercise for each of the six attitudes. Once you have determined your top two attitudes, the applications section later in the book will help put you in control of your career, communications, and relationships.

Theoretical Attitude Statements

Scoring Scale:
5=Always 4=Most of the time 3=Sometimes 2=Rarely 1=Never
(Circle One)

5 4 3 2 1   I greatly enjoy discovering, understanding, and ordering knowledge.

5 4 3 2 1   The pursuit of knowledge, identifying truths and untruths, motivates me.

5 4 3 2 1   I am good at integrating the past and present.

5 4 3 2 1   Many see me as an intellectual.

5 4 3 2 1   People who make emotional arguments without the facts frustrate me.

5 4 3 2 1   I have a keen interest in formulating theories and asking questions to assist in problem solving.

5 4 3 2 1   I am fulfilled by work that requires ongoing education as well as the use of prior knowledge.

5 4 3 2 1   Every time I am near a bookstore I want to stop in.

5 4 3 2 1   I use knowledge to convince others of my ideas, and I win arguments because of the facts I know.

5 4 3 2 1   I want to know just for the sake of knowing.

Now, add your circled score from each of the statements and write your total score for the Theoretical Attitude below. Your total will be from a minimum of 10 up to a maximum of 50. The higher the number, stronger your Theoretical Attitude.

THEORETICAL ATTITUDE SCORE
35–50: Strong Theoretical
25–34: Average Theoretical
10–24: Weak Theoretical

Strong Theoretical
Attitude: You have a passion for knowledge and the discovery of the truth. You tend to agree with most of the statements above.

Average Theoretical
Attitude:

Your drive for knowledge and the discovery of truth tends to be situational. You learn everything about specific topics. One or two of the other five attitudes will be your primary motivator.

Weak Theoretical
Attitude:

You are either negative or indifferent to knowledge and discovery of truth. When you hear someone laying out the facts, you may lose interest and tune out the discussion. Your desire to learn and know is highly situational. If you have a weak Theoretical Attitude, you will find your passion elsewhere in this chapter.

Listed below are more characteristics of the Theoretical Attitude. With a strong Theoretical Attitude, you will relate to many of them. If you do not, it may surprise you that people actually think this way.

- See the value of having good libraries and bookstores in every community.
- Have difficulty putting down a good book.
- Use knowledge to produce harmony with your surroundings.
- Extend projects beyond the boundaries for the sake of increased knowledge.
- Have the facts to support your conclusions.
- Dislike what you believe to be shallow social discussions and look for a deeper discussion.
- Enjoy informational television shows and shows where a mystery is unraveled.
- Expect a great deal of information before making a decision.
- Ask a great many questions: who, what, when, where, how, and why?
- Support educational programs in your city, community, and country.
- Have a willingness to learn about practically anything.

Do these sound a lot like you? If you don't have a strong Theoretical Attitude, you may still relate to some of the statements above but probably only in specific circumstances and situations.

The driving passion for the Theoretical Attitude is the discovery of knowledge and truth. You use your cognitive ability to discover, categorize, and systematize the truth. You are a walking gatherer, classifier, and searcher of knowledge. You always seek new truth, even perhaps at the risk of personal safety. How will this attitude affect your life and your actions? We will examine career issues, relationship issues, and communications as related to the Theoretical Attitude.

My research supports the conclusion that many people are in careers that do not bring them satisfaction, and they would leave that career if they could afford to make the change. Your vocation must fulfill your passion or you will not value your job. What are some of the careers that might fulfill the passion of the Theoretical Attitude?

• Research	• Computer Programming
• Education	• Statistics
• Computer Science	• Science
• Marketing	• New Product Development
• Law	• Medicine

As I have stated before, with a Theoretical Attitude you have a passion to know, to search and discover truth. By answering the questions below you will understand better how your social interactions are affected.

1. Do you believe education is very important and that educational programs will assist society in solving many of its problems?

2. Do you tend to dislike shallow social conversations and quickly move the conversation into deeper topics?

3. Do you believe a college education is a must?

4. Do you find yourself wanting to go new places and learn about new things? Do you have a passion for history and facts?

5. Do others often ask you for information? Even when you don't know the answer, do you have a desire to research it and find out? Are you viewed as a source of information?

6. Do many of the items you own have a story, a history that goes with them?

7. Are you viewed as an expert in a specific field?

8. Do those you most enjoy talking to fulfill your Theoretical need for knowledge and truth?

9. Do you tend to turn away from people who present their cases without the facts?

10. Do subjective discussions bother you?

Even in a social realm, you will have a desire to search out and know. Your Theoretical Attitude has an effect on the programs you believe are valuable and supportable and on the relationships you believe to be meaningful and worthwhile. When you look at a painting you will find that you want to know all about it. When you are presented with emotional issues, you will try to analyze them and explain them rationally. When you get into a discussion with someone, you will find that you can tear huge holes in a weak argument and that you enjoy intense discussion of the facts which leads to deeper learning. What a unique person you are! Driven in all aspects of your life to learn, know, and discover. You are a true explorer!

If you are attending the Olympic Gymnastics competition, you will want the discussion to be on gymnastics, not basketball. If someone tries to talk basketball with you at that particular time, you might even go so far as to ask them why they have even attended a gymnastics competition. The point is that to communicate with you, with your strong Theoretical Attitude, I must communicate in your arena, in your way, according to your attitude. Otherwise, you may quickly lose interest and move onto another discussion. **Note**: If I communicate with you according to what YOU value, you will find satisfaction in the conversation.

In the arena of sales, I greatly enhance my chances of getting you to buy if I package my presentation in your attitude. How? To sell to someone with a strong Theoretical Attitude, I would include the following in my presentation:

- History
- Research
- Questions
- Facts
- Manuals
- Problems, requiring your assistance

Plus, I would make sure I was totally objective and had covered all the bases before I made the presentation, knowing and respecting your ability to analyze, clarify, and dissect an argument.

Your attitude affects your valuing of life even in spiritual issues. In my database of people who have taken the attitudes assessments are questions about careers, social relationships, communication, success, and spirituality. Their answers were consistent with their dominant attitude. Some of those comments are:

- Regarding power: Knowledge is power.
- Regarding contentment: Understanding brings contentment.
- Regarding education: Having a little education only is dangerous.
- Regarding truth: A question answered leads to another question asked.

Experiences lead to beliefs. Beliefs cluster together into categories. The categories form a specific hierarchy of attitudes. Where would the world be without those who ask questions, analyze, clarify, and search out the truth? Those with the Theoretical Attitude are the ones who will discover new truth, attempting and proving new procedures that can better humanity and improve all of our lives.

You will not understand the Theoretical Attitude unless you listen carefully to others who are strong in this attitude. You will be amazed at these people. The amount of knowledge they have gained and their tremendous passion to learn more is ever present. Often I hear this statement: "But, I like to learn about things also and I don't have a strong Theoretical Attitude." You may like to learn, but do you have a passion to learn about everything? Probably not. If there is a mystery, are you driven to solve it, to learn the unknown, regardless of the field? A person with a strong Theoretical Attitude is well versed in many fields. There will be little knowledge that he or she is negative or indifferent to. Discuss, listen, and learn from them—their world will amaze you.

The Theoretical Attitude

The Tree of Knowledge

I sat on a hillside and looked at a tree.
Its intricate detail surrounded me.
How deep are the roots? How long has it grown?
How did it survive on the plain all alone?
What kind of tree is it? Who planted it there?
How many great people have breathed the same air?
Is there a stream flowing under the tree,
Coloring the leaves a deep forest green?
I sat on a hillside and looked at a tree.
Its intricate detail beckoned to me.
I'll stay here awhile, learn all that I can.
Then I'll walk closer—inspect it again.
Secrets untold will open to me
To know the unknown—all from a tree.

R. J. Widrick

With the Utilitarian Attitude, life is investment and return. The Utilitarian says, "I will make an investment of my time and resources if there is an adequate measurable return, not just in money but also in time."

Here's a personal example: Most Sundays, I attend church. There are two choices. I can go to the 7 A.M. or the 10 A.M. service. The 7 A.M. service is twenty minutes shorter because it does not include hymns or choruses. I attend the 7 A.M. service. My Utilitarian Attitude is that I am sure God would get no pleasure from my singing voice and I save twenty minutes. God is happy because he doesn't have to hear me sing and I'm happy because I get done sooner. That's the Utilitarian Attitude in action. My valuing of the service was connected to my desire for utility.

The passion of the Utilitarian Attitude is "what is useful" in all areas of life.

Let's assess your Utilitarian Attitude. Here again are ten statements for which you will need to circle a 5–1 response based on how well the statement describes you. Remember, there is no right or wrong answer.

Utilitarian Attitude Statements

Scoring Scale:
5=Always 4=Most of the time 3=Sometimes 2=Rarely 1=Never
(Circle One)

5 4 3 2 1   I evaluate things based on their utility and economic return.

5 4 3 2 1   I tend to move to practicality in all areas of life.

5 4 3 2 1   I am very conscious of the use of my time, achieving the most for the minute.

5 4 3 2 1   I desire an adequate return on any investment I make.

5 4 3 2 1   Wealth provides the needed security for myself and my family.

5 4 3 2 1   I am very future oriented.

5 4 3 2 1   Money and possessions are scorecards of my success.

5 4 3 2 1   I want to be rewarded accordingly for my time and effort.

5 4 3 2 1   I attempt to structure and control any economic dealings I have.

5 4 3 2 1   I tend to purchase things that have an investment value.

Now, add your circled score from each of the statements and write your total score for the Utilitarian Attitude below. Your total score will be from a minimum of 10 up to a maximum of 50. The higher the number, the stronger your Utilitarian Attitude.

UTILITARIAN ATTITUDE SCORE

35–50: Strong Utilitarian
25–34: Average Utilitarian
10–24: Weak Utilitarian

Strong Utilitarian
Attitude:
    Whether you realize it or not, many of your actions will be driven by investment and return of your time, talent, or resources. As you read on, think about investment and return, utility, and practicality.

Average Utilitarian
Attitude: You may be practical situationally, looking
                                       for return on investment only in specific
                                       arenas, but the Utilitarian Attitude is not your
                                       driving passion.

Weak Utilitarian
Attitude: You may react negatively when someone
                                       seeks return on investment, or you may be
                                       indifferent and not care. If you have a weak
                                       Utilitarian Attitude, you will find your
                                       passion elsewhere in this chapter.

Those with Utilitarian Attitudes are often misunderstood. Using my own strong Utilitarian Attitude for example: I always required accountability from my children. If they would ask me for money I would usually ask them to perform some task in return. Essentially my thinking was: If I provide you with that, what will you do for me?

This bothered me at times. I always seemed to have strings attached. Return on investment is very important to me because of my strong Utilitarian Attitude. I required accountability from my children and hopefully taught them that working hard in a given field will pay off in the end. However, I am learning that I do not always have to have a return on my investment. Because I understand my Utilitarian Attitude, I can also control the situation. I have found that I enjoy doing some things for people with no strings attached.

If you have a weak Utilitarian Attitude, you may have to learn to ask for a return on your investment. We have all seen what happens to children when they are given everything with no accountability. Businesses cannot exist if they are not profitable and do not have positive cash flow. The answer is to have balance. In business you need to give away brochures, products, and maybe even your time in order to gain exposure and let people experience your services. Everything cannot have a string attached. But, at some point, you have to charge a fair price for your services or you go out of business. In relationships people need accountability but sometimes we should do something nice for someone "just because."

Current research, regardless of the person's attitude, indicates that women do not ask for enough money, and this contributes to the fact that women are paid less.

In examining more of the Utilitarian Attitude characteristics you will see a tendency toward:

- Being able to apply resources creatively to solve a problem.
- Reject that which you consider to be a waste of resources or time.
- Futuristic thinking.
- Work long hard hours to gain financial security.
- Enjoy capitalistic endeavors.
- Plan your daily activities to best utilize your time.
- Give your cell phone number to only a few people to avoid excessive charges.
- Like to make deals based on investment and return.
- Want to advance quickly within your chosen profession.
- Desire incentive and bonus plans.
- Always expect something in return for services rendered or time given.

Where would we be if there was no accountability? All of the economies of the world are dependent upon investment and return. Every business or organization, even churches, need to use their resources wisely. A person with a strong Utilitarian Attitude has a passion to maximize available resources.

If you do not have a strong Utilitarian Attitude, you may not totally understand how they think or why they do what they do. Believe me, when you are trying to find the best use of resources to accomplish a task, a person with a strong Utilitarian Attitude will put together a scenario that you will not believe!

As we did with the Theoretical Attitude, we can also examine the flow of the Utilitarian Attitude through your career, social relationships and communication.

To be fulfilling, your career must be an extension of who you are. With a strong Utilitarian Attitude, you are driven by adequate return on investment. Your income or how you are paid for your services will be very important to you.

Here are some questions to answer—are they showing a strong Utilitarian Attitude?

1. How will you feel if you are in a career where there is no upward mobility?
2. How will you respond to a career where everyone, no matter how hard they work, gets the same minimal (two to three percent) raise each year?
3. What about a career where promotions are based on seniority?
4. Would you enjoy a career where, in order to make more money, you had to wait for someone to die, move, or retire?

On the other hand, think about a career where . . .

1. You are compensated for your efforts. Namely, you determine your paycheck based on your efforts.
2. You are afforded generous bonus and incentive plans based on performance.
3. You can move quickly in a small start up company where the boundaries are very casually defined.
4. You have control of your time and schedule and can work your days or nights as you see fit.
5. You can own your own business.
6. You can use creativity and futuristic thinking.

Which type of careers motivate you the most? With a strong Utilitarian Attitude, the second list above will best meet your passion. You may want to seriously consider owning your own business. You will definitely want a career that includes bonus plans, incentives, pay based on performance, and the ability to advance quickly. A career in a large well established firm might box you in too much, although a sales or sales manager position may fulfill your passions.

You have to have a return on investment of your time, talent, and resources. You may even study in a field requiring extensive education, such as law or medicine, as long as you are sure the return will be worth the investment of all the required education.

A word of caution. If you only find fulfillment of your attitude on the job, you could easily become a workaholic. You must find fulfillment of your attitudes both on and off the job.

In terms of your social and personal relationships, your Utilitarian Attitude can have an effect.

- Do you find yourself not wanting to do activities that you consider a waste of time?

- Do you, rather than fixing an item, just replace it because it is easier?

- Are practicality and utility a major factor in your purchases? Possessions? Clothing?

- When you pack for a trip, do you pack only what you need?

- Is it easy for you to hold people accountable?

- Do you lend your possessions or money without an expected return date?

- Can you make a little last a long time?

- Would you consider yourself a conserver of resources?

Here's a synopsis of an actual conversation between two business-women packing for a five day convention. One has a strong Utilitarian attitude and the other has a weak Utilitarian Attitude.

Debbie: Let me see, if I take these two dresses I can wear the same pair of shoes with both. These two will match these shoes. Penny, which ones should I take?

Penny: All of them. You can decide which ones you want to wear after we get there.

Debbie: Why would I pack them all when I don't need them? The banquet is on Saturday night, which dress should I wear?

Penny: Take all three. You can decide on Saturday night. I'm taking all of mine.

Debbie: I wouldn't even think of taking them all. It's not practical.

Penny: I wouldn't think of not taking them all. You're strange.

Debbie: What jewelry are you taking?

Penny: I'm taking my whole jewelry box.

Debbie: You're kidding. I would never . . .

Penny: You are hilarious! I take everything I need and then I make my choices when I'm there.

Get the picture? Many of our everyday interactions, agreements, and disagreements flow out of our attitudes. Adopting Penny's approach would drive Debbie crazy. It is a completely different way of thinking. And, can you imagine Penny having to choose between dresses before she left?

With a foundation of integrity, all of your communication should focus on a mutual benefit for both parties. Your communication should not result in a benefit to one party and loss to the other. To communicate with a strong Utilitarian Attitude, I would focus on return on investment. I would show what I wanted you to invest in resources and time and then demonstrate a factual realistic payback for services rendered. The payback doesn't have to be immediate; it just has to be adequate. Whether I am asking you to invest money or time, in order to gain your approval and involvement, there has to be a return on your investment.

An interesting observation is that society has wrongly implied that those who give their lives to others are in some way better or higher than those who are concerned about themselves. If you do not take care of your personal needs, you will not have the ability to take care of others. In business, if you are only interested in helping people and are not concerned about the bottom line, you will go out of business and be unable to help anyone.

If, on the other hand, all you care about is the bottom line, then you do not understand the importance of the people around you or the immense value of those who work for you.

In relationships, business or social, accountability is needed. Society today has moved away from accountability, much to our detriment. If your first passion is toward return on investment of your time and resources, then I would suggest you follow the advice of Zig Ziglar who stated: "You can get everything you want in life by helping others get what they want."

A Utilitarian Attitude creates a passion that requires fulfillment—it also requires balance. Utility may not be wise in all areas, which is exactly why we need around us people who think differently, to help mold us into all we can be.

Psychology recognizes something called "Premack's Principle." Essentially it states: "The reward comes after the work—or—the enjoyment comes after the pain."

As parents we have all used this one: "Do your homework and then you can play." This is the Utilitarian Attitude in action. All incentive plans are based on investment and return. All contracts are based on return on investment. What would happen to our economic structure if we eliminated any passion, personally or professionally, for return on investment?

With an understanding of each other, the Theoretical and Utilitarian can be friends and increase each other's value of life. Here's how:

1. Use knowledge to maximize resources and create new inventions.

2. Use resources, time, and money to increase and search out knowledge.

The Theoretical Attitude searches out and discovers knowledge. The Utilitarian Attitude applies it to the marketplace and to life, funneling some of the profits back into research and development.

The Utilitarian Attitude

The Tree of Utility

I sat on a hillside and looked at a tree.
Visions of grandeur surrounded me.
I saw houses and barns, ships tall and fast,
Cradles and tables, statues and beds.
The tree took these forms as I watched carefully
I saw how useful a tree can be.
To make all of life better, to bring my life joy
To produce new creations, jewelry, and toys.
I sat on a hillside and looked at a tree.
Visions of grandeur surrounded me.
I leapt into action to realize my dreams
Intensely, with passion, I ran toward the tree.
What a wonderful resource a resource can be.
To better my life—all from a tree.

R. J. Widrick

Do you have a strong Aesthetic Attitude? If you do, you will have a passion toward self-realization and self-actualization. You will also be in tune with and aware of your surroundings.

In a friend's house I saw a clock on the wall that had stopped running. "Why would you put a clock on the wall that doesn't work?" I asked. It made no sense to me. "Bill, the clock isn't on the wall to tell time. It is on the wall because it fits beautifully with the design of the room." You can imagine my consternation as a strong Utilitarian—the clock was supposed to give me accurate time. We were looking at the same clock but we both saw it differently. She valued the clock because it was beautiful. Beautiful or not, to me, the purpose of a clock is to tell me the time. Don't you agree? How many times in life do several people view the same picture and yet see something completely different? One values the experience and the next doesn't. Do you have a strong Aesthetic Attitude?

Always keep in mind that the six attitudes I am describing are not right or wrong. They have no morality. They are your way of viewing the world, and the passions that move you into action. Here's an opportunity to assess your Aesthetic Attitude.

Aesthetic Attitude Statements

Scoring Scale:
5=Always   4=Most of the time   3=Sometimes   2=Rarely   1=Never
(Circle one)

5 4 3 2 1   I desire and seek the finer things in life.

5 4 3 2 1   I am in a continual self-improvement process.

5 4 3 2 1   I enjoy and am aware of the beauty of my surroundings, which I like to complement my feelings.

5 4 3 2 1   I am very aware of my inner feelings.

5 4 3 2 1   I have a strong interest in the preservation of our natural resources.

5 4 3 2 1   Looking and feeling good is one of my goals.

5 4 3 2 1   I want harmony and balance in my life.

5 4 3 2 1   I invest time and money in self help material.

5 4 3 2 1   I am very creative.

5 4 3 2 1   I appreciate and look for the beauty in things and people.

Now, add your circled score from each of the statements and write your total score for the Aesthetic Attitude below; your total will range from a minimum of 10 up to a maximum of 50. The higher the number, the stronger your Aesthetic Attitude.

AESTHETIC ATTITUDE SCORE
35–50: Strong Aesthetic
25–34: Average Aesthetic
10–24: Weak Aesthetic

Strong Aesthetic
Attitude:

Your actions are driven by a passion for form, harmony, and beauty within and without, extending to your clothes, possessions, and surroundings. Your concerns about environment are very strong.

Average Aesthetic
Attitude:

Your passion for form, harmony, and beauty are situational only, and do not extend to the totality of your life. Other attitudes will drive your actions.

Weak Aesthetic
Attitude:

Your passions are found in one or two of the other attitudes, not in the Aesthetic. You tend to be negative or indifferent to the Aesthetic point of view. You should definitely invest time with someone who is strong in the Aesthetic Attitude to understand their viewpoint. If you have a weak Aesthetic Attitude, you will find your passion elsewhere in this chapter.

The Aesthetic Attitude continues to be one of the most fascinating for me to study because I do not see the world that way. My company publishes many training guides and behavioral assessments. I really struggled with the material. My staff urged me to make the materials look good, to invest money in artistic design and impressive graphics. The behavioral tools I had developed were excellent and well validated. I didn't see the need for investing large amounts of money and time to make them pretty. My world was viewed through the Utilitarian Attitude with a weak Aesthetic Attitude. The Utilitarian dominated my decisions. I have learned to change my thinking. My staff now has a budget to make our products look their best. When I see a completed project with an impressive Aesthetic appeal, my one rule is this: Don't tell me how much it costs!

Several people on my staff have strong Aesthetic Attitudes. Their way of seeing and valuing the world has been essential to the success of our marketing efforts. They understand an aspect of the business that is foreign to me.

The Aesthetic Attitude extends beyond wanting nice and beautiful things. It is a complete life mindset. It is a way of looking at the world. With a strong Aesthetic Attitude you are immersed in your surroundings, actively interacting with your environment to become all you can be, with an intense passion for self development. Following are a few more Aesthetic characteristics. A person with an Aesthetic Attitude will tend to:

- Work for less money as long as the surroundings are aesthetically pleasing.
- Have difficulty working in bleak surroundings.
- Appreciate the finer things in life and strive to get them.
- Be good with colors, arrangements or design.
- Strive toward harmony and unity within your physical and relational world.
- Be empathetic to the feelings of others.
- Dislike and avoid those who are insensitive to your feelings.
- Be subjective in your decision making process, going more with your instinct.
- Notice changes in familiar surroundings, such as furniture moved, a new picture on the wall, flowers planted, etc.
- Be aware of fashion, dressing in good taste for success.
- Be involved in several ongoing self-help programs.
- You may be susceptible to purchasing the newest and the latest products.

With a strong Aesthetic Attitude it would be fitting to say, "Your world speaks to you." In a world where success is often labeled in terms of money and possessions, a person with a strong Aesthetic Attitude may easily define success as, "To be . . ."

Many people with strong Aesthetic Attitudes work in the beautiful ski resorts of Vail or Aspen. They are willing to do minimal wage jobs in order to live and play in a natural winter wonderland. They come from all over the world, drawn to a place that allows them to be who they are. The passions of your attitude demands fulfillment, being directly connected to your self-esteem.

What if you, with a strong Aesthetic Attitude, have a career where:

- Creativity is not encouraged or allowed?
- Your surroundings are gray and bleak?
- You are not allowed freedom of expression?
- Everybody must wear the same uniforms? Or adhere to a dress code that doesn't allow for individuality?
- You might be asked to "pour chemicals down the drain"?
- Top management makes all the decisions and your ideas cannot be discussed?
- There is no color in the environment?
- There is a lack of harmony in the environment?
- Everything seems to be unstructured? Chaotic?

If you are in a work environment that is inconsistent with your attitudes, it doesn't mean that there is anything wrong with you. With a strong Aesthetic Attitude, money becomes only a means to fulfill your desire for beauty, harmony, and form. You may work long and hard to enjoy the finer things in life. However, once you have attained the beautiful in life (your own standard) money becomes necessary only to maintain your standard.

When you leave a job that is not in line with your attitudes, you will feel as if a huge load dropped from your shoulders. The new job will excite you and bring out the passions of who you are. You will find that even if the money is less on the new job, your value of life will increase.

Money has several beliefs tied to it. One, which may not be true at all, is this:

If I have money → I will be happy → the more money I have → the happier I will be.

The lives of men and women throughout history have shown that this statement is not true. Over 40 percent of high level executives would change their careers if they could replace the money. What does this mean? It means that these executives are zeroing out in careers they do not have any passion for—would you like to work for one of them? Maybe you are one of them?

There's a great phrase: "If you are not doing something you love, change what you are doing." With a strong Aesthetic Attitude, your chosen field needs to allow for the following:

- Creative expression
- Self-actualization and self realization
- Freedom of ideas

Your surroundings should be aesthetically pleasing. What career fields are in line with a strong Aesthetic Attitude? Here are some suggestions:

• Arts	• Photography
• Interior Decorating	• Environmental Careers
• Forest Service	• Fashion Design/Modeling/Jewelry
• Architecture	• Music
• Drama	• Writing

With a strong Aesthetic Attitude, the location of your job can also fulfill your passion. In other words, you may not really care for the job but love where you work. Many people have jobs in the national park services because of the beauty of the environment. To be able to work in the magnificent surroundings of the Grand Canyon could fulfill your passion for form, harmony, and beauty.

Your attitude is not worn like a garment that you can take off or put on. It is an integral part of who you are.

- Do you strive to look good in all you do and own?
- Do you have a passion to experience new things, new activities, new places?
- Is most of your conversation related to the subjective (feeling) element of an issue?
- Do problems with personal relationships bother you?
- Do you notice changes in your surroundings? An example:

A young woman was lying on the psychiatrist's sofa, very nervous and agitated. "Relax," he said. The woman replied, "How do you expect me to relax when I know the sofa is supposed to be over there?"

- Do you have an ability to aesthetically order a room, knowing exactly where each piece of furniture should go? Each picture?
- Do you find yourself negatively judging people based on their appearance?
- Do you find yourself valuing people and places based on their appearance?
- Is the car you drive aesthetically pleasing?

How do I communicate with you in terms of your Aesthetic Attitude in search of form, harmony, and beauty?

- Focus on the big picture
- Use descriptive words and phrases, simile and metaphor
- Focus on harmony and balance
- Discuss the subjective element and the experience
- Ask you to describe the picture "the way you see it"
- Identify areas of imbalance and focus on solutions
- Visualize . . . "picture this . . ."
- Focus on self improvement.

When communicating with a strong Aesthetic Attitude, I can also focus on the means to the end. For example, you may not want to do the job but you do appreciate the finer things. Therefore, you may do the work to attain them.

The person with an Aesthetic Attitude can bring a "slowing down" to the world, an appreciation of the environment. Take the time to enjoy the beauty that the strong Aesthetic brings to the world; I have learned to do just that.

So, here we are:

The Theoretical Attitude:	A passion to search out and discover the truth.
The Utilitarian Attitude:	A passion for utility and return on investment.
The Aesthetic Attitude:	A passion for beauty, form and harmony.

Do any of these sound like you? Remember, your two top attitudes drive your actions and we still have three more to discuss. Next is the Social Attitude which is just as it sounds—a passion to realize the potential of others and eliminate hate and conflict in the world.

The Aesthetic Attitude

The Tree of Beauty

I sat on a hillside and looked at a tree.
A vision of all that I strive to be.
Form a young shoot she has grown tall and strong,
To a beautiful tree, her goal all along.
Her branches are woven, a fabric of leaves
The intricate pattern so lovely to see.
I take in the beauty, the form and detail
I embrace her color, her breath I inhale.
Expressions of joy I can hardly contain
She speaks out to me, calling my name.
An aroma of senses pours out in my soul
A picture of form, harmonious detail.
Dressed in glorious hues, green and brown
A garland of fruit forms a queenly crown.
I sat on a hillside immersed in the tree,
A vision of all that I strive to be.

R. J. Widrick

With a strong Social Attitude you will find fulfillment in helping and serving others and eliminating hate and conflict in the world. Your deep concern for the welfare of others will motivate you to freely pour out your time, talent, and resources to better humanity.

In order to assess your Social Attitude, please read each of the ten statements below and circle a 5–1 response, based on how well the Social statement describes you.

Social Attitude Statements

Scoring Scale:
5=Always 4=Most of the time 3=Sometimes 2=Rarely 1=Never
(Circle one)

5 4 3 2 1   Eliminating hate and conflict in the world is one of my passions.

5 4 3 2 1   I have a passion to improve the whole of society.

5 4 3 2 1   I am generous with my time, talents, and resources when I see someone in need.

5 4 3 2 1   I am empathetic to those who are hurting.

5 4 3 2 1   In business I will sacrifice bottom line profit for a more people oriented decision.

5 4 3 2 1   I tend to avoid confrontation if it will harm the relationship.

5 4 3 2 1   I believe people should support charities.

5 4 3 2 1   In business I want everyone to receive the most that their money can buy.

5 4 3 2 1   Saying "no" to others is difficult when people need my time and talents.

5 4 3 2 1   I blame the system more than the individual and work to change the system.

Now, add your circled score from each of the statements and write your total score for the Social Attitude below. Your total will be from a minimum of 10 up to a maximum of 50. The higher the number, the stronger your Social Attitude.

SOCIAL ATTITUDE SCORE
35–50: Strong Social
25–34: Average Social
24–10: Weak Social

Strong Social Attitude: You have a passion to better humanity, to invest your time, talents, and resources in helping the world become a better place. You will find tremendous fulfillment and value life as you pursue social types of activities and careers. You may not understand others who are not like you.

Average
Social Attitude: You have a passion to assist others only situationally, under given conditions and circumstances, such as family needs or specific causes, but not a passion for the whole world.

Weak Social Attitude: You may react negatively to social causes believing them to be a waste of resources and time. You will find your passion and value of life in two of the other five attitudes. As you read on, seek to understand the Social Attitude and how it plays out in society so you will know how to communicate effectively with such a person. If you have a weak Social Attitude, you will find your passion elsewhere in this chapter.

Did you score a strong Social Attitude? You will find new satisfaction in life as you make decisions in line with your Social Attitude. On inspection you will find that many of your conflicts are the result of your Social Attitude being attached or unfulfilled.

With a strong Social Attitude you will tend to:

- Invest your time, talents, and resources even if there is no return.
- Support charitable causes and have a hard time saying "no" to requests for time and money.

- Give to others, even to your own detriment.
- Get angry with others who seem to have too much focus on the dollar and too little on the people involved.
- Believe corporations have no concern for people regardless of what they say.
- Under-value your talents and services and give them away for virtually nothing.
- Take on causes that cannot be won.
- Promote fairness to people in all areas of life.
- Preserve the classics in music, art, and literature so that future generations can enjoy them.
- Help the homeless.
- Be involved in projects that will impact society.

Can you relate to any of these statements? All of them come from real people who have taken assessments and scored a strong Social Attitude.

Does this touch a chord? "Companies don't care about people anymore, only about the bottom line. Decisions should be made with a people focus ahead of the almighty dollar."

Fred works in a company of 1,000 people that is in the process of downsizing. With a strong Social Attitude, he experiences a great deal of stress working in such an environment. All that is within him cries out for the concerns of the people, nothing within him understands the bottom line and the necessity of downsizing. The stress and struggle are magnified because Fred is a manager who must oversee the layoffs.

With a strong Social Attitude, your career must let you focus on the people element. You may find a strong aversion to many aspects of the corporate world, specifically the emphasis on profits. However, organizations that encourage personal development and promote empowerment of the workforce will tend to motivate you.

With a strong Social Attitude, how will you respond to a career where:

- The focus on the bottom line is the highest priority, ahead of people?
- You are not in a position to help others?
- Decisions are made that you believe hurt people?
- You are rewarded for sales goals?

- Where you have to close the sale?
- The beliefs of the organization are different from yours?
- You are not empowered to make decisions that help others?

Can you feel it? With a strong Social Attitude, even considering these job characteristics will cause your stomach to tighten. Everything inside you will resist this type of job. So, don't get in one. Regardless of how much you are paid!

One further question to think about. Why would an employer want to place you in a position that doesn't fit who you are?

The Saguaro cactus dots the landscapes of Arizona, thriving on the hot desert climate. What would happen to the same cactus if it is planted in upstate New York? People would think you were crazy to plant them there. They would not be able to grow because they are ill-suited to that climate. Nor would the maple tree of New York survive in the desert of Arizona. Your unique personal design requires that you be "planted" in soil to sustain and support your growth and development. Am I saying that certain attitudes fit certain careers better than others? Yes, indeed!

Whatever you choose as a career, make sure it has activities in line with your Social Attitude. Here are a few examples:

- Medicine/Health Care
- Social Work
- Charities
- Education
- World Relief Organizations
- Ministry
- Counseling
- Consulting
- Customer Service
- Sales and Service of Existing Accounts

You may be able to think of others. With your strong Social Attitude you need to become part of the interviewing process. Not only are the prospective employers interviewing you, you need to interview them, making sure that the job fulfills your passions and desires.

Here's a story: Allen worked in sales. His sales manager was concerned that he seemed unable to close the sale. He met people easily and made them feel at home right away but he couldn't close the sale. Why? We assessed Allen and he showed a strong Social Attitude. He loved meeting the people and helping them but everything inside of him resisted the sale. He kept thinking, "Do they really need this? Can they afford it? Am I really helping them?" Respecting Allen's people ability, the manager became very creative. He had Allen continue to use his tremendous ability to meet people and make them feel welcome. Once Allen established a good relationship, he was assisted in the closing by another salesperson who enjoyed the negotiation aspect. Allen still successfully works in sales having found a way to fulfill his Social Attitude.

- Are you bothered when people around you seem overly focused on their own interests and not the interests of others?
- Are you quick to help others who are in need of your time, talents, and resources?
- Do you get taken advantage of because of your giving nature?
- Do you see more potential in others than they see in themselves?
- Do you give to others even at your own expense or to your own hurt?
- Do you invest more in a relationship than the other party?
- Do you tend to stay in a bad relationship too long?

Here's a tough one:

- Do you try so hard to save the world that you neglect the needs of yourself and your family?

There are many accounts of doctors and nurses who, during a plague, pushed themselves so hard that they ended up getting sick and dying. It would have been better if they had been willing to rest, keep their strength and therefore, maintain their usefulness. With a strong Social Attitude, you may be so focused on others that you neglect your own personal needs or safety. Be aware of that drive in your activities and relationships. You may be willing to give up the very air you breathe because others need it more. To make a difference you need to care for yourself and make your own needs a priority as well. Remember this commandment we all learned at an early age? "Love your neighbor as yourself." The emphasis was always placed on neighbor, however, the love for your neighbor is based on the fact that you love yourself first.

If you are talking with someone who has a strong Social Attitude, my suggestion is to focus on:

- Making society better
- Helping people
- Bettering the world
- Realizing the people potential

With a strong Social Attitude, you will not care about investment and return (Utilitarian) or form, beauty, and harmony (Aesthetic) or a discovery of knowledge (Theoretical). Why would I communicate to you in any of those "flavors" if I know you are going to be negative or indifferent to them? But, if I demonstrate how my ideas are going to assist you in helping people achieve their potential and making the world a better place, you will buy into my ideas. Your passions will move you into action. I form a common bond, a unity of purpose with you as I see the world through your eyes, your Social Attitude.

Sun Tzu, in *The Art of War*, called the ability to adapt—genius. The solid foundation of communication has to be win/win. If anyone loses in the communication, then that is manipulation. With a win/win perspective, communication to you according to your attitude becomes exciting, fun, and rewarding.

The person with a strong Social Attitude invests in humanity, to make the world a better place. Where would we be without: famine relief organizations, health care clinics, food shelters, the American Red Cross, the United Way, shelters for abused women and children, and the list goes on . . . those with a strong Social Attitude have greatly enriched society and enhanced the world to make it a better place.

In looking at the four attitudes we discussed so far, the Theoretical, Utilitarian, Aesthetic, and Social—each with their own unique view of the world—put them all at a table and do you think we would have conflict? I think so.

The Social Attitude

The Giving Tree

I sat on a hillside and looked at a tree.
I imagined how helpful it could be.
To eliminate conflict and hate in the world
To help others achieve their potential for good.
Lofty branches lend a shade from the sun—
An oasis for travelers on their way home.
A swing dangling from the branches so high
Lifts playful young children up to the sky.
A community picnic would bring folks together
To know one another, then all would be better.
Together we all could plant more of these
So others could enjoy the beauty of trees.
I sat on a hillside and looked at a tree
I know how helpful it would be
To bring out the best, to show each one he can—
To benefit greatly the family of man.

R. J. Widrick

To someone with a strong Traditional Attitude, life has a purpose and a higher meaning; this person embraces a group of beliefs that leads to a system for living. The passion of the Traditional Attitude is the search for the highest meaning in life.

Below are ten statements reflecting the Traditional Attitude, circle a number from 1–5 which best reflects your position.

Traditional Attitude Statements

Scoring Scale:
5=Always 4=Most of the time 3=Sometimes 2=Rarely 1=Never

(Circle one)

5 4 3 2 1   I have a system for living and want others to follow my system.

5 4 3 2 1   Rules and regulations should be adhered to.

5 4 3 2 1   I tend to support organizations that hold the same beliefs I do.

5 4 3 2 1   I can be overly rigid in evaluating others against my standards.

5 4 3 2 1   I will be more helpful to others who share my beliefs.

5 4 3 2 1   My conscience is my guide.

5 4 3 2 1   I place a high value on living in tune with a higher purpose.

5 4 3 2 1   I believe my system for living is right and when challenged I will attempt to "convert" the person to my system.

5 4 3 2 1   I have found a "rule book" for life and I follow it.

5 4 3 2 1   If I believe strongly in a cause, I will champion it.

Now, add your circled score from each of the statements and write your total score for the Traditional Attitude. Your total will be from a minimum of 10 up to a maximum of 50. The higher the number, the stronger your Traditional Attitude.

TRADITIONAL ATTITUDE SCORE

35–50: Strong Traditional
25–34: Average Traditional
10–24: Weak Traditional

Strong Traditional
Attitude: You believe you have found a system for living or even a "rule book" that will lead you and others to the highest meaning in life. You tend to reject beliefs which do not fit in your system.

Average Traditional
Attitude: You probably do not have a set system for living and may be in the process of investigating several systems, adopting, and rejecting beliefs from each.

Weak Traditional
Attitude: You may react negatively to someone who believes they have found a system to live by. Your opinion may be, "just don't force your beliefs on me!" Your actions are driven by one or two of the other attitudes. If you have a weak Traditional Attitude you will find your passion elsewhere in this chapter.

For some insight into the Traditional Attitude, consider that Edward Spranger originally named it the Religious Attitude. I can best describe it as a river of principles that flow into all areas of your life. Your activities, career, and choices emanate from these principles. The Traditional Attitude believes that if you adhere to your principles you will achieve the highest meaning in life. Any belief that is contrary to the principles is rejected. Every experience is judged in comparison to the river of principles.

With a strong Traditional Attitude you will tend to:

- Believe you have found a system for living that works and is right.
- Judge others positively or negatively according to your principles.
- Believe your way leads to the "divine" and follow it religiously.
- See a higher meaning in life, nature, art, people, music, and all other aspects of life.
- Be drawn to causes, careers, and activities that promote the principles you believe in.
- Explain all issues from your belief perspective.
- Be concerned about humanity and its direction.
- Be protective of the traditions you hold dear.
- Actively seek to convince others of your viewpoint.
- Be involved in religious and charitable organizations.
- Be conservative, slow to change.

- Be idealistic even though your ideals may seem unrealistic.
- Believe there are absolutes, right and wrong clearly defined.

The strong Traditional Attitude believes our words and actions have meaning and that we are called to a higher purpose in life. They believe in accountability and are willing to offer answers to the purpose and meaning of life. With a strong Traditional Attitude you have intense beliefs about birth, life, death, and beyond. You offer us hope—you may also condemn us. You will always take a stand.

With the strong Traditional Attitude, beliefs are all connected into a complete system for living. No belief is tolerated that does not fit into the system. This Attitude will cause you to speak boldly and confidently, which will sometimes cause you problems. To help you properly understand your strong Traditional Attitude, I am going to break it down into two types:

The Protector: The Traditional Protector believes in his way of life and passionately protects it. Not necessarily wanting to convert others, the protector is seeking a place where he can live out his beliefs without others taking away his rights. The Amish are an example of this attitude.

A person can be religious and not be strong Traditional. That is why I changed the term to Traditional. The key element that makes the person strongly Traditional is a "closed system" of beliefs; this person lives with a confidence that the main questions of life such as "Why am I here?" have been answered.

The Idealist: The Idealist also has a system for living, a closed loop of thinking (not a closed mind), but the desire is to achieve the ideal meaning of life and to change the world to their point of view.

The strong Traditional Attitude appears often in the epic movies of our time. Men and women, armed with nothing more than a vision, challenged the powers that be and lifted humanity to new heights, accomplishing unheard of deeds.

Your strong Traditional Attitude will lead to a consistent life, you will live within the boundaries of your belief system.

In terms of career, there could be trouble in a job because what you might be asked to do, you could interpret as going against your beliefs. Your strong Traditional Attitude demands that you be in an environment consistent with your beliefs. Your beliefs are more important to you than your job, money, or material possessions. Employers who hire you need to understand that your belief system is stronger than the paycheck or the job. Often running your own business according to your beliefs will offer you the most satisfaction. Many Traditionalists have gone into social work and the ministry, while others have found a safe place in the corporate world.

With a strong Traditional Attitude you need to know two things about your relationships.

1. You will enjoy and appreciate people who believe as you do.
2. You will tend to not accept people who do not believe as you do.

Most relationships fail because of a conflict in beliefs and values. What happens when both people believe their system to be right and the two systems are not in harmony? Conflict. You must be careful that your strong belief system does not lead to being closed-minded. Here's some food for thought: "I can accept the near right and I can accept the far right. I do have trouble with the ALWAYS right."

I am not suggesting that you change your belief system or that you compromise. But, before you make a judgement on ideas and beliefs that seem contrary to your own, take time to hear the person out and find out why they believe what they do. This course of action will expand your thinking. You may even find that their beliefs can be intertwined with your system without compromise. If you are open-minded and teachable, you can enjoy richer relationships than you thought possible. As you listen to others with differing viewpoints, you will find that they are more apt to listen to you.

To communicate with a strong Traditional Attitude, it is important to:

- Take the time to understand their beliefs.
- Understand their purpose and vision.
- Make sure your presentation adheres in all aspects to their belief system.

If my communication does not fit within your belief system, I can then follow one of two other paths:

- If you are teachable, we can still talk and even agree to disagree.
- If you are not willing to listen, I need to walk away respectfully, always leaving a door open for future communication.

All six attitudes see the world a different way. Are you beginning to see why there is so much conflict in the world? In the family? As you study the attitudes, remember again that the top two drive your actions. Very few people are driven by just one of the six attitudes.

The Traditional Attitude

The Spiritual Tree

I sat on a hillside and gazed at a tree.
A symbol of life, it speaks out to me.
Its arms reach up and embrace the sky
Directing all men to a power on high.
From the roots to the trunk to the branches and leaves
A heavenly structure, a system complete.
A symbol of parts that work as a whole
A unified team, achieving the goal.
All trees will be measured by this standard so tall
This tree is the pattern, the mold for them all.
I sat on a hillside, I know what I see.
Before me, in glory, the one perfect tree.

R. J. Widrick

Coming up now is the Individualistic Attitude. It is unique in that it must channel through one or two of the other five attitudes, each which has a single focus or a specific world view. The passion of the Individualistic Attitude is to achieve the highest power or position, to control others, or control their own destiny and independence.

Life is a chess game of strategic relationships and key alliances leading to increased power and positions of leadership. Certain people have a predisposition to be leaders. In these positions of leadership, they will find their passion and destiny. However, position and power are of no value without someone to lead or a cause to champion.

So the question is asked, "Whom do I lead?" The Individualist desires to lead people. Power and position do a leader no good unless he has people to lead. The Individualist will find an arena where a leader is needed, where his direction and guidance will be valued and will flourish. The arena which allows the Individualist to "flex his leadership muscle" will be one of the other five attitudes.

Here is how the Individualistic Attitude can use the other five attitudes:

Through Theoretical: I will become an expert in my field. People will follow me because I am the guru in my field.

Through Utilitarian: I will gain position through the attainment of wealth. I will attain wealth by maximizing my available resources.

Through Aesthetic: I will be a leader in helping others become all they can be. I will use my creative abilities to achieve form, harmony, and beauty in the world.

Through Social: I will lead people to support humanitarian causes. I will invest my time, talent, and resources into making the world a better place.

Through Traditional: I will point people to a higher path in life. People have questions of existence and purpose. I will study and answer those questions, causing people to follow me.

The Individualistic Attitude, unlike the other five attitudes, maintains a flexibility. This person can be happy in many areas, as long as there is the ability to advance and achieve. You will find the Individualist in sales, religion, art, and education. The soil that allows the Individualistic Attitude to flourish is advancement and position. I would also speculate that the Individualistic person will make dramatic switches in career to advance their position.

Power has no inherent morality. Like a gun on the table, it takes on the morality of the person who picks it up. Corrupt men corrupt power—

good men use power wisely. The world needs men and women of integrity who attain and use leadership positions for the good of humanity. Let's take a look at your Individualistic Attitude in the following ten statements below. Circle a 5–1 response which best represents your position.

Individualistic Attitude Statements

Scoring Scale:
5=Always 4=Most of the time 3=Sometimes 2=Rarely 1=Never
(Circle one)

5 4 3 2 1   I like people who are determined and competitive.

5 4 3 2 1   I believe that when the going gets tough, the tough get going.

5 4 3 2 1   It is important for me to be in control of my own destiny.

5 4 3 2 1   I strive to maintain my individuality.

5 4 3 2 1   I believe I can direct the destiny of others.

5 4 3 2 1   I want to be recognized for my accomplishments.

5 4 3 2 1   I believe "If at first you don't succeed, try again."

5 4 3 2 1   I will work long and hard to achieve the position and influence I want.

5 4 3 2 1   I tend to believe "The end justifies the means."

5 4 3 2 1   I tend to play whatever "cards" necessary to gain control over a situation.

Now, add your circled score from each of the statements and write your total for the Individualistic Attitude. Your total will be from a minimum of 10 up to a maximum of 50. The higher the number, the stronger your Individualistic Attitude.

INDIVIDUALISTIC ATTITUDE SCORE

35–50: Strong Individualistic
25–34: Average Individualistic
10–24: Weak Individualistic

Strong Individualistic
Attitude:

Life is a chess game to you. Advancing your career and moving yourself into leadership positions puts you on a positive course. You have a passion to control your personal life and direct the lives of others.

Average Individualistic
Attitude:

You may have a desire to be a leader in a specific situation. Your primary passion comes from one or two of the other attitudes.

Weak Individualistic
Attitude:

You may react negatively to those who seek to advance their position—to people with strong ego and strong control. You probably distrust those in power. You will also find your passion in one or two of the other attitudes. If you haven't found your passion by now, you are one of the few unique individuals who have so much balance in their lives that they are not really passionate about anything. Or, you may be going through a process of trying to discover who you are.

As stated before, the Individualistic Attitude is the most flexible of all six attitudes. It finds fulfillment in one or two of the other five attitudes. The passion of the Individualist is achieving the highest power and position. With a strong Individualistic Attitude you tend to:

- Gravitate to positions of leadership in organizations.
- Seek out the limelight.
- Resist being micro-managed or controlled, preferring freedom of operation.
- Desire a fast pace toward advancement.

- Have a low tolerance for people who do not challenge themselves.
- Be seen as too strong and overpowering.
- Form strategic relationships and key alliances.
- Be a visionary, adhering to beliefs that will advance your cause.
- Be willing to use power to accomplish a purpose.
- Have an ability to see the "big picture" and how the puzzle interlocks.
- Gather and unify resources to accomplish a purpose.
- Surround yourself with a "brain trust" to make sure all bases are covered.

The Individualist is often misunderstood. It does not mean that you are power hungry or always jockeying for position and taking "center stage." Nor does it mean that you are good or bad. It means you have a passion to lead, to direct your destiny and the destiny of others. You will persist, overcoming obstacles and rising from failures until you fulfill that passion. Many of the greatest men and women in history had a strong Individualistic Attitude.

The flexibility of your Individualistic Attitude allows for enjoyment of virtually any career that meets your passion for advancement and achievement of leadership positions. Whatever the position, you will require a relatively fast career path, with opportunities to lead or excel. Any career that does not offer you advancement and recognition will prove unfulfilling to you.

How passionate would you be about a career with the following characteristics?

- Advancement based on seniority.
- Slow or no career pathing.
- Base weekly salary, equal raises for all regardless of performance.
- Little or no recognition.
- An established company, with little freedom of operation.

Or would you rather have:

- Advancement based on performance.
- Control over your own destiny.

- Bonus and incentive plans.
- Rewards and recognition.
- Freedom of operation and schedule.
- Quick paced career paths.
- Room at the top for you.

With a strong Individualistic Attitude, everything about you will resist the first type of career. The second list puts you on that positive course because it is an extension of who you are, a fulfillment of your Real Self.

Keep in mind that many of the people with strong Individualistic Attitudes we have worked with have had problems in their relationships. The problems stemmed from the fast pace Individualists keeps to achieve their goals. In your relationships you may have to work on putting people first.

People issues get sacrificed on the way up the ladder of success. Your desire to lead can take you to great heights and your effect on humanity can be tremendous. At times the position will conflict with people and you will have to make choices. Your natural tendency will be to secure your position instead of taking care of your people. Remember this: you cannot lead unless you have someone to follow you. It is people who put other people into positions of power. It is people who take people out of those positions, either by vote or by violence. Therefore, you must never lose your focus on what is best for your people.

With your desire for leadership and your desire to control your own destiny and the destiny of others, you need to examine your motives for each relationship, making sure that it is good for all parties involved. This focus will enhance your ability to move forward and will put a spotlight on those people who are not willing to work with you.

In order to communicate with you or to move you into action, it would be important to focus an the following:

- Benefits to you.
- Key relationships that will be formed.
- Advancement of position.
- Attainment of power.
- How you will look.
- Your goals and dreams.
- Fast pace of goal attainment.

Even if you know what I am doing, it will be acceptable because it is who you are. That's the beauty of a proper, validated understanding of human behavior. People enjoy being communicated with in their own attitudes. Why would we talk to a strong Individualist about helping others or making money? That is not their passion.

An example of the Individualistic Attitude: John is a salesperson, a very good one. He often attends training seminars, but after one of these, the trainer did not hand out certificates. "Where's my certificate?" John asked. "I frame all my certificates and put them on the wall of my office." When customers came into John's office, they saw three walls filled with plaques, awards, and certificates. The message John wanted to convey? I am a professional. I am the best. This is the Individualistic Attitude in action.

The Individualistic Attitude

The Tree of Power

I sat on a hillside and looked over the plain.
I felt like a king, power coursed through my veins.
I stood there in majesty, none taller than me.
Except for a massive, majestic old tree.
It stood there in grandeur defying my claim,
Its arms stretched out farther, challenging my name.
Its power just awed me, I took a step back.
How can I employ this massive asset?
I could make toys and jewelry and produce even more.
I could sell all the lumber and give to the poor.
I could study the tree, every cranny and nook
Make note of my findings and publish the book.
I could capture its beauty with paper and pen.
Or show it reveals the divine unto men.
I sat on a hillside and looked at a tree.
I desire to transfer its power to me.
I know my mission, I know that I can
With the tree as my ally, I'll win with my plan.

R. J. Widrick

Six people sit and look at a tree. Each has the potential to be a winner in life and to make a difference. All have their own dreams and their own plans. The first sees the tree of knowledge. The second sees the useful tree. The third sees the tree of beauty. The fourth sees the giving tree. The fifth sees the spiritual tree and the sixth sees the powerful tree. All find value in the tree that is an extension of their Real Self.

Suppose we elected them all to a "tree committee" and they had to decide what to do with this tree. Can you see the conflict that would happen? It's easy to walk the other way when we are in conflict. It is much more difficult to learn to understand and work together.

People all over the world benefit from this study of attitudes; companies teach their people to understand each other better by knowing more about their personal views of the world—so more can be accomplished when you know who and what you are dealing with, right?

The top two attitudes in your hierarchy drive your behavior. Which have you decided are your dominant attitudes? I believe you will find it much easier to "walk with another when you are able to understand each other."

10

How to Find Passion in Your Career and Activities

After assessing each of the six attitudes, you discovered which attitudes are your strong, average, or weak ones. Go back to them and find your total scores for each attitude and write that score in the space below:

_____ Theoretical Attitude

_____ Utilitarian Attitude

_____ Aesthetic Attitude

_____ Social Attitude

_____ Traditional Attitude

_____ Individualistic Attitude

The closer the number is to 50, the stronger the attitude. Rank each of the attitudes below, from highest to lowest score. The two highest scores will be your dominant attitudes. In case of a tie for second, go back to the specific attitude and think carefully as you answer each question again.

Score	Attitude
_____	_____
_____	_____
_____	_____
_____	_____
_____	_____
_____	_____

If your career, relationships, and communication align with the two top attitudes on the list above, you experience a passion for life, a desire to move into action. Now with a more accurate picture of your Real Self, you will be in control of the value of life. With a better understanding of others, you will be able to increase their value of life as well, helping them make decisions in line with their attitudes.

Change is a process. You have to decide whether you are willing to start this process. Are you willing to invest time to understand how your attitudes affect your life?

Suppose that you want to move from Point A to Point B.

A – – – – – – – – – – – – – **B**

We know that change is related to pain and reward. Judy Suiter, a consultant friend in Atlanta, states: "People change when the pain of where they are at is greater than the potential pain of change." If you want to move from Point A to B, two things will cause you to move. There will be pain at Point A or there will be a reward at Point B. Either or both will cause you to move into action. If the pain or reward is great enough, you will move. Let me show you how you can be in control of your life. How you can make decisions that will enhance your valuing of life.

By looking at each of the attitudes in the chart on the next page, you will see how the pain or reward of the change process works with the attitudes. If your current environment is not fulfilling your top two attitudes, *pain* will be the result. If you encounter a new environment that fulfills the passions of your top two attitudes, you will have an inner desire to move to the new environment, and *reward* will be the result.

A → → → B

	PAIN	REWARD
Theoretical Attitude	No ability to learn	Continuing education
	Shallow Work	Research
	Everything understood	Mysteries; new truth
Aesthetic Attitude	Lack of form and harmony	Form and harmony
	No personal growth	Self-improvement plan
	Stifling of creativity	Creative expression
Utilitarian Attitude	Wasted resources	Maximize resources
	No return on investment	Return on investment
	Seniority/no incentives	Incentives/bonus plans
Social Attitude	Self-promotion	Investment in others
	Non-people focus	People projects
	Downsizing	Teamwork with a goal
Traditional Attitude	Beliefs that conflict yours	Unity of beliefs
	Chaos	Order
	Self-serving philosophy	Betterment of mankind
Individualistic Attitude	No advancement	Leadership opportunity
	Seniority	Quick advancement
	Controlled environment	Opportunity to control

If there is *pain* at Point A and/or a *reward* at Point B that fulfills your top two attitudes, you will experience a desire to move. If the reward or pain increases enough you will definitely move. We are beings who desire meaning in our lives. We move naturally to a place where we can be valued and have high self-esteem and we move naturally out of an environment where we are not valued. You cannot hate your job and love it at the same time. If you love your job, it is because your job fits who you are.

11

The Discovery Process

Change is related to pain and reward. Place a mark in the previous chart next to your top two attitudes to always remind yourself what your strongest attitudes are. If your environment does not fulfill the passions of those two attitudes, you will experience dissatisfaction, either at work, in relationships, or in communication. Possibly all three!

Tennessee Williams once said, "There is a time for departure even when there's no certain place to go." The discovery process begins when you realize it is time for departure from the present environment. This process, as taught by Judy Suiter, consists of five steps that I think are good tools to use. The first step is an *awareness* that something is bothering you. You just simply know that something is wrong in your inner world. By talking with a friend or colleague, you can begin to shed some light on what it is that bothers you, which then moves you to the second step, *understanding*. As you desire to understand what bothers you, you will gain clearer insight by talking with others. Discussion with others is essential to understanding the problem and seeing it clearly. Once understood, you can begin to develop a solution even though it may not be an easy one. Now comes the hard question—will you accept it? *Acceptance* means you acknowledge that you are the one in control of your life, and if you want it changed then you must change it yourself. You have to supply the motivation. You now understand the *problem* and you know the solution. Will you take responsibility for your life and solve your problem? It's your choice.

You will probably have to make hard choices and new *commitments*. Yes or no? If yes, then let's see some *action*. I can know your commitment by watching what you do, not what you say. If I see action then I know you have really made a commitment. If there is no action, you make no change and you seem unwilling to move, it's because the pain and reward is not great enough. Unfortunately, either you or someone else has to increase the pain or the reward.

Earlier I expressed the belief that personal growth and development is also a process. It takes perseverance and patience. Very few things happen instantaneously.

In the process of achieving our Potential Self, having a partner to share with is crucial. Remember these: "Two heads are better than one" and "Many hands make light work." My research shows that teams always out-perform the individual. The solutions that come from group consensus are almost always better than the individual.

To achieve your Potential Self, keep in mind the benefits of working in partnership with someone. They can be a great source of encouragement on the days that you "just don't feel like running the race."

I cannot assume that you want the same things I do. Without taking the time to understand your motivations and objectives, the stage is automatically set for conflict and failure. If I take the time to understand your attitudes, understanding your driving passions will follow.

A story is told of an elderly man who owned several acres of undeveloped land. Certain developers recognized his land as a perfect site for a shopping mall. Offer after lucrative offer was refused by the old man. No matter how much money was put in front of him, he would not sell.

A new developer approached the man regarding the property. He also wanted to build a shopping mall. Aware of the previous refusals, the developer tried to understand why he wouldn't sell. In their conversations, he realized the old man had more than enough money and had very little attachment to the property. However, he also discovered in these conversations that the elderly man had a deep concern for the welfare of his granddaughter and that he wanted to be remembered after he died.

This developer presented a plan to the old man whereby the mall would be named in memory of him with a memorial statue in the center court. A trust fund would be established from the purchase of the property that would adequately take care of the granddaughter. The elderly man agreed and sold the property.

That is a simple story but a powerful message. Understanding the other person must be a primary focus in your communication. You cannot give someone what they want if you do not know what they want. An understanding of the six attitudes puts you in control of the conversations you participate in. By asking questions and listening, you will know which two attitudes are the dominant ones, and then you can work toward a positive solution for you both.

Changing our methods of communication using the six attitudes provides us with tools that will enhance every aspect of life.

On the following pages are some exercises related to the six attitudes. You might like to try a few of them just to test your comprehension of all we have talked about in this book.

Relationship Exercises

Look at the example exercise below and then try your own luck at some of the others.

Example: A married couple discusses family finances.
Husband: Strong Utilitarian, Strong Theoretical
Wife: Strong Social, Strong Traditional

Possible Conflict: The husband will want to invest money while the wife may want to support charitable organizations in line with her beliefs. She will be freer in giving than he prefers her to be. She may remind him of how much he spends on continuing education and how much time he is away from home taking night classes which could have an adverse effect on their family life.

Note: A mutually beneficial solution starts with an understanding of the attitudes. By understanding that these are not right and wrong issues, the couple can work out a solution that allows them both to fulfill their desires.

Here are some exercises for you to try.

1. The CEO and her Vice President discuss an upcoming layoff.
CEO: Strong Utilitarian
VP: Strong Social

Possible Conflict: _____

_____
_____
_____

Possible Solutions: _____

_____

_____

_____

2. Two women, both good friends and equally qualified, are considered for a high level promotion. Both are strong Individualists.

Possible Conflict: _____

_____

_____

_____

Possible Solution: _____

_____

_____

_____

3. Two men discuss religion. One is strong Theoretical and the other is strong Traditional.

Possible Conflict: _____

_____

_____

_____

Possible Solution: _____

_____

_____

_____

The following communication exercise might be an interesting activity for you to try.

1. Of all the people you interact with regularly, which one is the most challenging and difficult to get along with? _____

_____

2. What is this person's occupation? _____

_____

_____

3. List some of the outside activities or organizations this person belongs to: _____

   _____

   _____

   _____

   _____

   This person's career and activities can give you insight into their top two attitudes.

4. Does this person seem to have a passion for their career?   Yes   No

5. Which of this person's outside activities is this person passionate about?

   _____

   _____

6. Based on their career and outside activities, as well as your conversations with them, circle what you believe to be their top two attitudes.

Theoretical	Aesthetic	Utilitarian
Social	Individualistic	Traditional

7. Do you think this person is in a positive cycle in their career and outside activities? List your reasons why or why not.

8. Is there a conflict between your top two attitudes and this person's?
   Yes   No

Your top two attitudes: _____

This person's top two attitudes: _____

9. What are the causes of conflict between you and this person? _____

   _____

   _____

   _____

   _____

Now I'd like you to do a similar process for yourself:

1. What is your occupation? _____

2. List some of the outside activities or organizations that you belong to:

_____

_____

_____

_____

_____

3. Do you have a passion for your career? _____

_____

4. Which of your outside activities are you passionate about? _____

_____

_____

_____

_____

5. Based on your career and outside activities, circle what you believe to be your top two attitudes

Theoretical	Aesthetic	Utilitarian
Social	Individualistic	Traditional

6. Do you feel as if you are in a positive cycle in your career and/or outside activities? List your reasons why or why not. _____

_____

_____

_____

_____

_____

This particular exercise is an opportunity to view a conflict situation with tools that can make communication much more manageable.

12

What I Know Now

All the previous chapters have been linked together by the desire to help you find your Real Self and to look at your career and your relationships in life. I want you to be able to find a career that matches your passion. You have also discovered ways to find out if your passion is met off the job instead of at work, and if you work at your present job only to have money to enjoy that passion outside of the workplace. Hopefully you now know that there is a career out there to match your passion—you just have to look for it.

Here's an example: There was a lady who worked for me. During the discovery process she discovered that her passion really dealt with plants and animals—she had a high Aesthetic Attitude. She came to me one day and asked if she could cut back her hours because she didn't have enough time to enjoy her garden or animals. Some time later, she again approached me to ask if she could return full time because she had decided to go back to college to get a degree in interior design and needed the money to pay for tuition. She was fulfilling her passion. Interestingly, she was so passionate about this new career that when she enrolled in two classes, she purchased the required books and had them completely read before classes even started! The discovery process helped her realize her desire—"I know who I am and where I am going."

You, too, could discover your passion and it could give you new life and more energy than you would ever believe possible.

So, get yourself a yellow pad of blank paper, a beverage of your choice, and find the right environment to kick back and REALLY think about your career. List all the activities that you enjoy doing and look forward to each day. Then list all the activities that cause you stress, frustration, and make a knot in your stomach.

If you find yourself in the wrong career, start looking now for a career that will let you do the type of activities that will energize you and make you feel good each day of your life.

Don't let self-limiting beliefs stop you! Many people believe that once they are trained to be an engineer, they must remain an engineer for the rest of their working life. That is tunnel vision and many of those individuals are in the wrong career. They have made choices that seemed right at the time, and somehow their need for security forces them to remain in the present career. No matter what career you prepared yourself for, you can still change and start over. My observation has been that when companies downsize or have layoffs, it is the fortunate ones who are laid off—they have a chance to start over.

Take some action steps once you have found a career that excites you. Interview people who are already in it and find out how they prepared to enter that specific career. What you'll discover is that they, too, probably started out in another direction and then changed to something that gave them purpose and energy.

Now that you have given your career a thorough examination, it is time to look at your relationship with your significant other in the same way. Find a spot where you can both sit down, share some time together, and visit about your similarities and differences. What activities do you both like? Do you share these activities? What don't each of you like to do? Coping with stress is relatively easy if you know why you have the stress, so spend some time on these points. Through the discovery process you can discern and acknowledge those differences and find ways to share satisfying time doing them. If you really enjoy sports and your partner enjoys the theatre—consider, what's three hours in an evening sharing something with a partner that you know is a nurturing experience for them? Rather than complain or resent the time spent at the theatre, you might consider the fact that you have shared an important experience and built a bridge of understanding between yourselves, and my guess is that your partner will be more than willing to face that next baseball game with you! This is a process to do with your children, your friends, and your working associates as well.

The choice is yours. You can choose to discover who you are and what you should be doing or you can go on as you are—the success discovery can take you through this journey.

If you *know* your Real Self, *understand* your Real Self, and *value* your Real Self, you have accomplished a successful discovery process. Just remember this: people who don't know themselves cannot help you discover yourself.

If I knew then what I know now, my life and career would have moved at a different pace and in different ways. You can choose to either look back or look at today. By choosing to look at today—you can change your course with confidence.